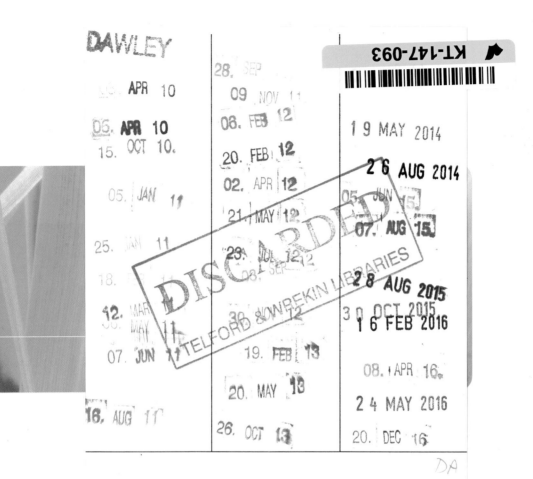
Please return/renew this item
by the last date shown.
Books may also be renewed by
phone and Internet
Telford and Wrekin Libraries

PEARSON
Prentice
Hall

Harlow, England • London • Ne[...]ong Kong
Tokyo • Seoul • Taipei • New De[...]ris • Milan

PEARSON EDUCATION LIMITED

Edinburgh Gate
Harlow CM20 2JE
Tel: +44 (0)1279 623623
Fax: +44 (0)1279 431059
Website: www.pearsoned.co.uk

First published in Great Britain in 2009

© Joli Ballew 2009

The right of Joli Ballew to be identified as author of this work has been asserted by her in accordance with the Copyright, Designs and Patents Act 1988.

ISBN: 978–0–273–72348–6

British Library Cataloguing-in-Publication Data
A catalogue record for this book is available from the British library

Library of Congress Cataloging-in-Publication Data

Ballew, Joli.
  Laptop basics in simple steps / Joli Ballew.
      p. cm.
  ISBN 978-0-273-72348-6 (pbk.)
  1. Laptop computers. I. Title.
  QA76.5.B2623 2009
  004.16--dc22
                        2009009526

Microsoft product screen shots reprinted with permission from Microsoft Corporation.

10 9 8 7 6 5 4 3 2 1
13 12 11 10 09

Designed by pentacorbig, High Wycombe
Typeset in 11/14pt ITC Stone Sans by 3
Printed and bound in Great Britain by Ashford Colour Press Ltd, Gosport, Hants

The publisher's policy is to use paper manufactured from sustainable forests.

Laptop Basics

In Simple steps

Joli Ballew

Use your computer with confidence

Get to grips with practical computing tasks with minimal time, fuss and bother.

In Simple Steps guides guarantee immediate results. They tell you everything you need to know on a specific application; from the most essential tasks to master, to every activity you'll want to accomplish, through to solving the most common problems you'll encounter.

Helpful features

To build your confidence and help you to get the most out of your computer, practical hints, tips and shortcuts feature on every page:

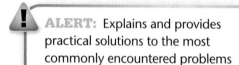

ALERT: Explains and provides practical solutions to the most commonly encountered problems

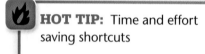

HOT TIP: Time and effort saving shortcuts

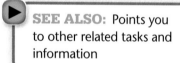

SEE ALSO: Points you to other related tasks and information

DID YOU KNOW? Additional features to explore

WHAT DOES THIS MEAN?

Jargon and technical terms explained in plain English

Practical. Simple. Fast.

in Simple steps

Dedication:

For Mom and Papa John, may you both rest in peace.

Author acknowledgments:

I just love writing for Pearson Education, and these *In Simple Steps* books prove it. Three books in almost as many months! It's wonderful working with Steve Temblett, Laura Blake and the rest of the gang. It's not often I find a team that works so well together.

I'd also like to acknowledge my agent, Neil Salkind, who works hard for me always, and my family, Dad, Jennifer, and Cosmo. I wish my mom could be here to see these books; she would have enjoyed them. You may see her in a few of the pictures here.

in Simple steps

Contents at a glance

Top 10 Laptop Problems Solved

Contents

2 Computer essentials

3 Vista essentials

6 Pictures, music and media

7 Getting online and surfing the Internet

9 Share data and printers

10 Change system defaults

11 Stay secure

12 Travelling with a laptop

13 Maintain your laptop

14 Fix problems

Top 10 Laptop Problems Solved

Top 10 Laptop Tips

Tip 1: Change the background

 Right-click an empty area of the desktop.

 Click Personalize.

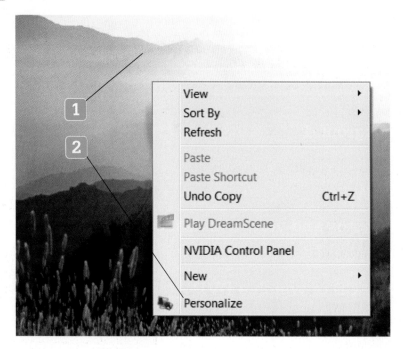

1

2

View	▶
Sort By	▶
Refresh	
Paste	
Paste Shortcut	
Undo Copy	Ctrl+Z
Play DreamScene	
NVIDIA Control Panel	
New	▶
Personalize	

 Click Desktop Background.

Personalize appearance and sounds

Window Color and Appearance
Fine tune the color and style of your windows.

Desktop Background
Choose from available backgrounds or colors or use one of your own pictures to decorate the desktop.

Screen Saver
Change your screen saver or adjust when it displays. A screen saver is a picture or animation that covers your screen and appears when your computer is idle for a set period of time.

4 For Location, select Windows Wallpapers. If it is not chosen already, click the down arrow to locate it.

5 Use the scroll bars to locate the wallpaper to use as your desktop background.

6 Select a background to use.

7 Select a positioning option (the default is the most common).

8 Click OK.

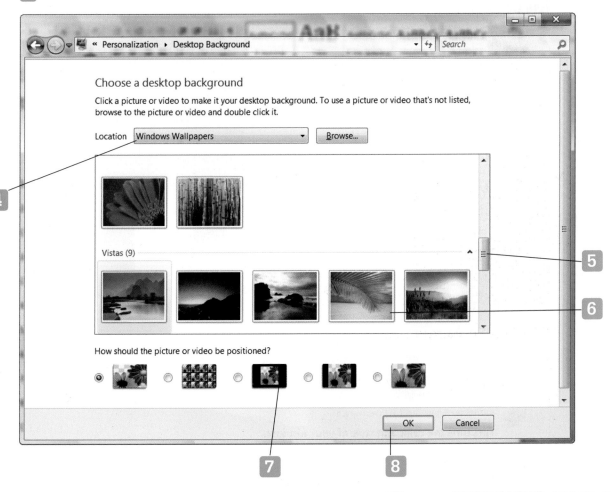

Tip 2: Use Flip 3D

1 With multiple windows open, on the keyboard hold down the Windows key.

2 Click the Tab key once, while keeping the Alt key depressed.

3 Press the Tab key again (making sure that the Alt key is still depressed) to scroll through the open windows.

4 When the item you want to bring to the front is selected, let go of the Tab key and then let go of the Alt key.

ALERT: If Flip 3D doesn't work, or if you get only Flip and not Flip 3D, either your PC does not support Aero or it is not configured to use it.

Tip 3: Turn on and off WiFi

1 Open Mobility Center.

2 Click Turn wireless off to disable WiFi.

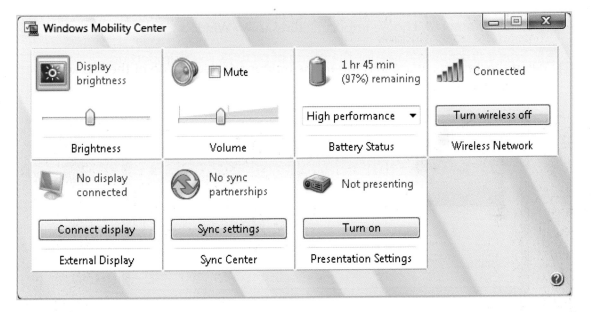

3 Click Turn wireless on to enable WiFi.

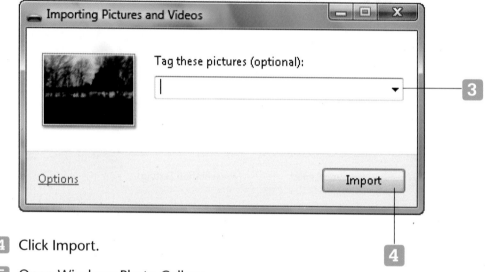

Tip 4: Upload digital photos and view a slideshow

1 Connect the device. If applicable, turn it on.

2 When prompted, choose Import Pictures using Windows.

3 Type a descriptive name for the group of pictures you're importing.

4 Click Import.

5 Open Windows Photo Gallery.

6 Expand any folder that contains pictures.

7 Click the Play Slide Show button. Wait at least three seconds.

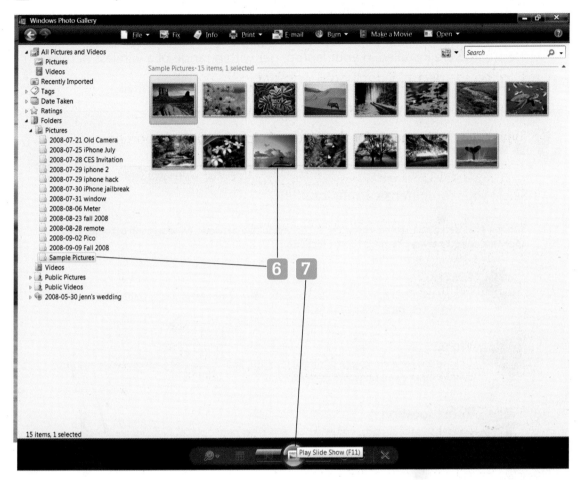

8 To end the show, press the Esc key on the keyboard.

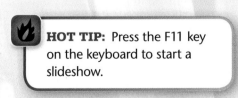

HOT TIP: Press the F11 key on the keyboard to start a slideshow.

Tip 5: Join a network

1 Connect physically to a wired network using an Ethernet cable or, if you have wireless hardware installed in your laptop, get within range of a wireless network.

2 Select Home, Work or Public location. (If necessary input credentials.)

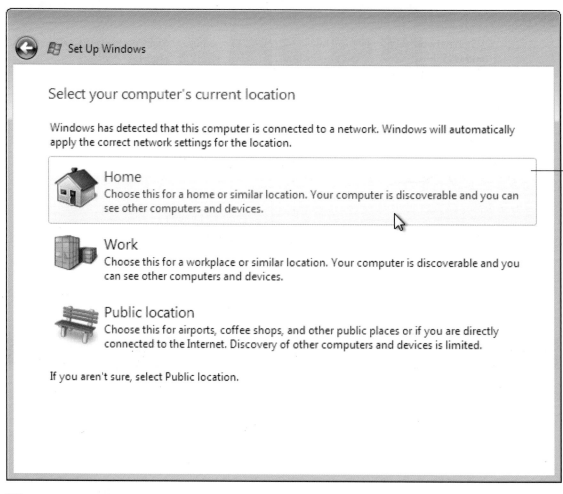

3 If you aren't prompted, Open the Network and Sharing Center.

4 Under Sharing and Discovery, click the down arrow next to Off by Network discovery. It will become an upwards arrow.

5 Click Turn on network discovery unless it is already turned on.

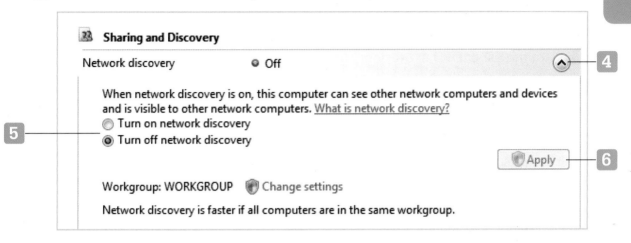

6 Click Apply.

7 Click the X to close the Network and Sharing Center.

Tip 6: Listen to a music CD or watch a DVD

1 Find the button on the laptop that opens the CD/DVD drive door. Press it.

2 Place the CD or DVD in the door and press the button again to close it.

3 When prompted, choose Play DVD movie using Windows Media Player, Play DVD movie using Windows Media Center, or Listen to music CD using Windows Media Player.

Tip 7: Watch, pause and rewind live TV

1 Open Media Center.

2 Move one click to the right of recorded TV and click live tv.

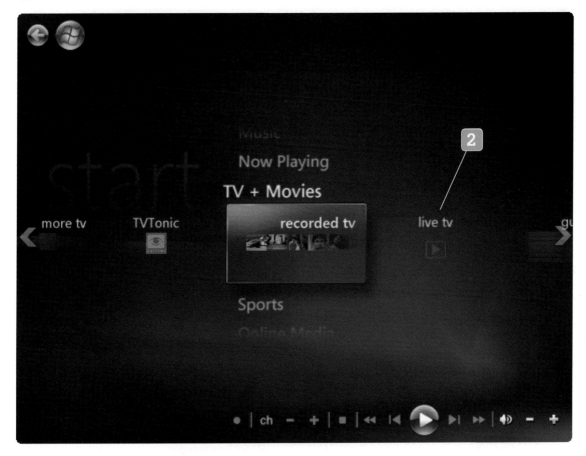

3 Position the mouse at the bottom of the live TV screen to show the controls.

4 Use the controls to manage live TV.

Tip 8: View and reply to an email

1 Click the Send/Receive button.

2 Click the email message to read it.

3 View the contents of the email.

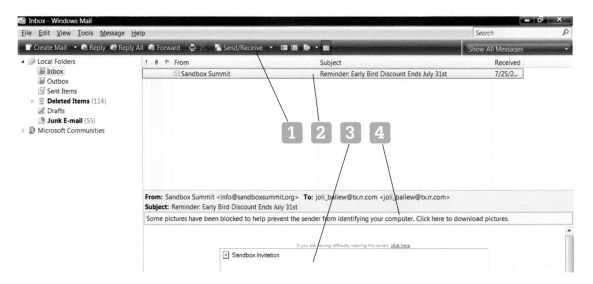

4 If you can't see the pictures in the email, click the yellow bar.

5 Click Reply.

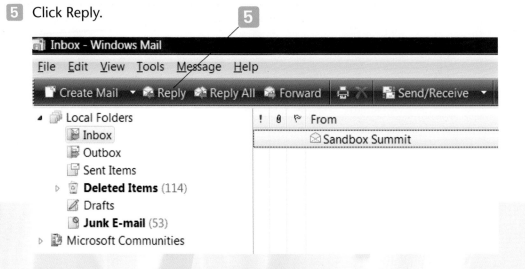

6 In the To: field, type the email address of the recipient.

7 Type a subject in the Subject field.

8 Type the message in the body pane.

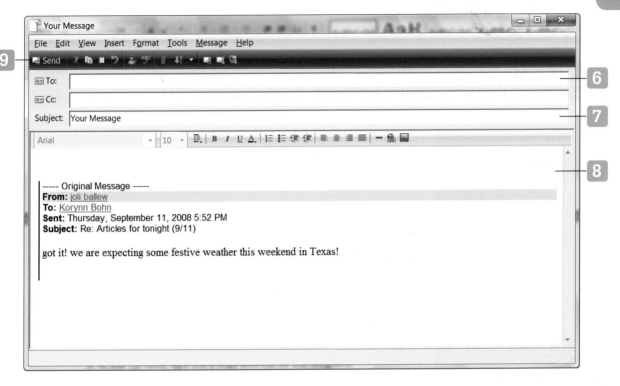

9 Click Send.

Tip 9: Change AutoPlay settings

1 Click Start.

2 Click Default Programs. (It's on the Start menu.)

3 Click Change AutoPlay settings.

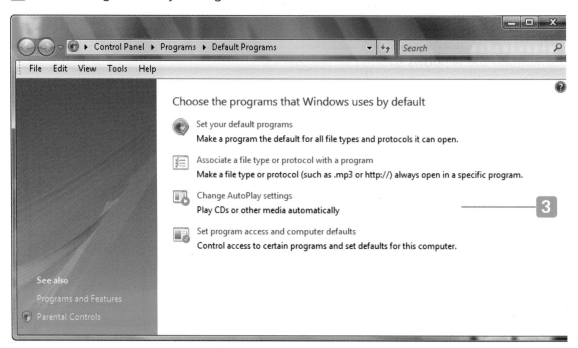

4 Use the drop-down lists to select the program to use for the media you want to play.

5 Click Save.

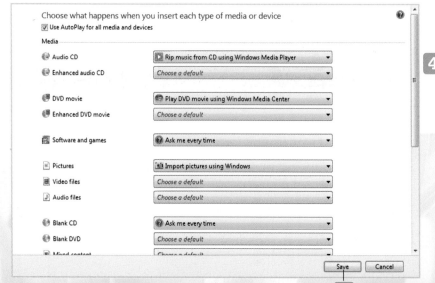

Tip 10: Back up data to an external drive

1. Click Start and click Computer.

2. Locate the external drive. (Leave this window open.)

3. Locate a folder to copy.

4. Position the windows so you can see them both.

5. Right-click the folder to copy.

6. While holding down the right mouse key, drag the folder to the new location.

7. Drop it there.

8. Choose Copy Here.

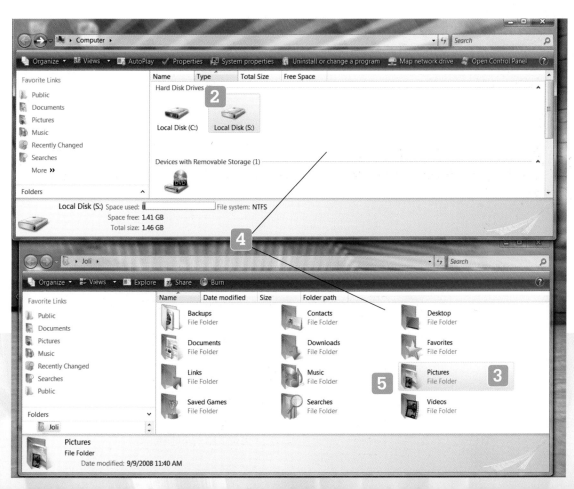

1 Explore your laptop

Introduction

A laptop has ports located on its outside, similar to what you'd expect to see on a desktop PC; there are Ethernet ports, USB ports, and a place to plug in external speakers and headphones, among other things. There's usually a CD/DVD drive too. The keyboard offers the usual array of keys, including Function and Page Up and Page Down keys. Laptops come with laptop-specific hardware, including a power button on the keyboard, a bay to hold the battery, and specialised configurable keys that you can personalise.

Once you've started your laptop, a process known as 'booting up', you'll find it has Windows XP, Windows Vista or Windows 7 running on it. These are both operating systems, and they allow you to operate your computer. In this book, I'll assume that your new laptop comes with Microsoft® Windows Vista, since this is a very popular operating system.

Plug in the power cable

A power cable is the cable that you use to connect the laptop to the wall outlet (power outlet). When you connect the power cable to both the laptop and the power outlet, the laptop will use the power from the outlet and charge the battery at the same time. When you unplug the laptop from the power outlet, the laptop will run on stored battery power.

 HOT TIP: Leave the laptop plugged in when you can, that way the battery will always be fully charged when you need it.

1 Locate the power cord. It may consist of two pieces that need to be connected.

2 Connect the power cord to the back or side of the laptop as noted in the documentation. You may see a symbol similar to the one shown here.

3 Plug the power cord into the wall outlet.

 HOT TIP: If your new laptop did not come with a booklet, visit the manufacturer's website and search for a user's guide.

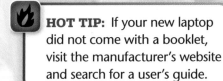 **DID YOU KNOW?**
You can connect and disconnect the power cable at any time, even when the computer is running.

Access and use USB ports

USB ports, or universal serial bus ports, offer a place to connect USB devices. USB devices include mice, external keyboards, mobile phones, digital cameras and USB flash drives.

1 Locate a USB cable. The USB cable's length and shape depend on the device, although one end is always small and rectangular.

2 Plug the rectangular end of the USB cable into an empty USB port on your laptop.

HOT TIP: Here's the universal symbol for USB:

3 Connect the other end to the USB device.

4 Often, but not always, you'll need to turn on the USB device to have Vista recognise it.

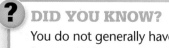

DID YOU KNOW?
You do not generally have to 'turn on' USB storage units, like flash drives.

HOT TIP: FireWire, also called IEEE 1394, is often used to connect digital video cameras, professional audio hardware and external hard drives to a PC. FireWire ports are larger than USB ports and move data more quickly.

Locate and use Ethernet ports

Ethernet, also called RJ-45, is used to connect a laptop to a local network. If you have a cable modem, router or other high-speed Internet device at home, you'll likely use Ethernet to connect to it.

1 Locate an Ethernet cable. They are often blue in colour, although they can also be grey, white or something else.

2 Connect the cable to both the PC and the Ethernet outlet on a router or cable modem.

HOT TIP: An Ethernet cable looks like a telephone cable, except that both ends are slightly larger. Here's the universal symbol for Ethernet:

? DID YOU KNOW?
When looking for an Ethernet port on your laptop, look for an almost square port. The Ethernet cable will snap in.

Connect external speakers or headphones

If there are any external sound ports, you'll probably see three. Most of the time you have access to a line-in jack, a microphone-in jack and a headphones/speaker/line-out jack.

1 If necessary, plug the device into an electrical outlet (speakers) or insert batteries (portable music players).

2 If necessary, turn on the device.

3 Insert the cables that connect to the device into the laptop in the proper port.

4 If prompted, work through any set-up processes.

	Line-in jack
	Microphone-in jack
SPDIF	Headphones/speaker/ line-out jack with S/PDIF support

WHAT DOES THIS MEAN?

Line-in jack: Accepts audio from external devices, such as CD players.

Microphone-in jack: Accepts input from external microphones.

Headphone or speaker jack: Lets you connect your laptop to an external source for output, including but not limited to speakers and headphones.

? DID YOU KNOW?

Line-in jacks bring data into the laptop; line-out jacks port data out to external devices such as speakers and headphones.

Locate additional ports

You'll probably see other ports not mentioned here, depending on the make and model of your laptop. You may see ports for a modem, external monitor, FireWire, serial, DVI and media card slots.

1 Turn the laptop and view all sides of it.

2 View the ports not mentioned here.

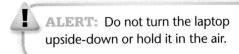

ALERT: Do not turn the laptop upside-down or hold it in the air.

3 Refer to your user's guide to explore these ports. Here is a serial port:

WHAT DOES THIS MEAN?

Kensington lock slot: Used to connect the laptop to a lock to prevent it from being stolen.

DVI port: DVI stands for Digital Video Interface. DVI is a video interface technology that is used to maximise the quality of flat panel LCD monitors. Most new, high quality video cards come with the older VGA connection as well as the newer DVI output port. Connecting using a DVI port requires you to also purchase a DVI cable. A DVI port is used to connect the laptop to a television set or other DVI device.

S-video: S-video is another type of interface technology. With this technology, the video signal is sent through a single cable but split into two signals, one for brightness and one for colour. When used to send a signal to a television, the result is a sharper and crisper picture. S–video is used to connect the laptop to a television or other display that also offers s-video connectivity.

SD card slots or card readers: Used to accept digital memory cards found in digital cameras and similar technologies.

ExpressCard: Used to insert an ExpressCard where you can expand your laptop's capabilities by offering additional ways to connect devices. ExpressCards are often used to offer wireless capabilities.

AV-in: Accepts input from various audio/video devices.

RF-in: Accepts input signal from digital TV tuners.

Locate, insert or remove the battery

There are several items that have to do with the battery, and they're likely all located on the underside of your laptop. Before you turn the laptop upside-down to look at them, make sure you turn off the laptop and unplug it.

1 If the computer is turned on, click the Start button on the Windows desktop. If the computer is not turned on, skip to Step 4.

2 Click the arrow shown here.

3 Click Shut Down.

4 Unplug the laptop from the wall outlet and remove the power cable. Set the power cable aside.

5 Carefully turn the laptop upside-down and place it on a desk or table.

6 Locate the battery bay and open it.

7 Unlatch the battery latch.

8 Remove or install the battery.

9 Lock the battery into place.

10 Secure the latch.

11 Close the battery bay door.

> **WHAT DOES THIS MEAN?**
>
> **Battery bay:** This holds the computer's battery. Sometimes you have to use a screwdriver to get inside the battery bay; other times you simply need to slide out the compartment door.
>
> **Battery release latch:** This latch holds the battery in place, even after the battery bay's door has been opened. You'll need to release this latch to get to the battery.
>
> **Battery lock:** This locks the battery in position.

Locate the power button and start Vista

Before you can use your laptop you have to press the power button on your laptop to start Windows Vista.

1 If applicable, open the laptop's lid.

2 Press the Start button to turn on the computer.

? DID YOU KNOW?
Starting a computer is also called 'booting' it.

! ALERT: If you ever have trouble starting Windows Vista, during the boot-up process hit the F8 key on the keyboard. You can then choose from various start-up options, such as 'safe mode'.

! ALERT: It takes a minute or so for the computer to start. Be patient!

? DID YOU KNOW?
Most of the time the power button is in the centre of the keyboard, at the very top.

Activate Windows Vista

If this is your first time starting Vista, and you're using a new laptop, you'll be prompted to enter some information. Specifically, you'll type your name as you'd like it to appear on your Start menu (capital letters count), activate Windows Vista and, if desired, register your copy of Windows Vista.

1 Follow the directions on the screen, clicking Next to move from one page of the activation wizard to the next.

2 When prompted to register, remember that registration is optional. You can skip this part.

3 When you have activated Vista, wait a few seconds for Windows Vista to initialise.

4 Click the Start button at the bottom of the Windows Vista screen to view your user name.

ALERT: To activate and register Windows Vista during the initial set-up, you'll have to be connected to the Internet. Alternatively, you can use the phone number provided to activate over the phone. If, during set-up, no connection to the Internet is found, a screen will appear with a phone number to call Microsoft to activate the product over the phone. The phone number is provided by Microsoft, and the user calls it, and then reads the required information to the person answering the phone. The person then activates the software manually (vs. activating automatically over the Internet).

ALERT: It's important to know that, although activation is mandatory, registration is not.

? DID YOU KNOW?
Activation is mandatory. If you do not activate Windows within the 30-day time frame, Windows Vista will lose all functionality, except for its activation process.

? DID YOU KNOW?
Usually you can press Enter on the keyboard to activate Next on the screen.

? DID YOU KNOW?
When you register, you offer personal identification about yourself, including your email address.

Use the touchpad

When you open your laptop for the first time, you'll likely see a device for moving the mouse, usually a touchpad or trackball. You'll use this to move the mouse around the screen.

HOT TIP: Double-click the left touchpad button to execute a command, and click once to select something.

1. Place your finger on the touchpad or trackball and move it around. Notice that the cursor moves.

2. If there are buttons by your laptop's touchpad, generally the left button functions in the same way as the left button on a mouse.

3. The right button functions in the same way as the right button of a mouse.

4. If there is a centre button, often this is used to scroll through pages. Try clicking and holding the button to move up, down, left, or right on a page.

HOT TIP: Right-click the left touchpad button to open context menus to access Copy, Select All and similar commands.

HOT TIP: Keep your fingers and hands clean when using the touchpad as it has a sensitive surface.

Locate specialised keyboard keys

Most laptop keyboards have more than a few universal keys. Much of the time, these keys offer the same things across makes and models. For instance, pressing F1 almost always opens a Help window for the open application.

1 With the laptop turned on and running, press the F1 key. Often this opens the Welcome Center (and sometimes Help and Support).

2 Press the Windows key. This often opens the Start menu.

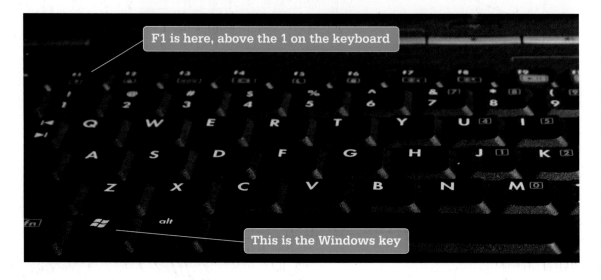

F1 is here, above the 1 on the keyboard

This is the Windows key

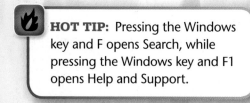

HOT TIP: Pressing the Windows key and F opens Search, while pressing the Windows key and F1 opens Help and Support.

Access configurable keyboard keys

All of the laptops I've seen recently come with specialised buttons that you can configure. These often include buttons such as Email, Web Browser, Bluetooth and Music Player, among others. Press these keys to open their related programs.

ALERT: Each manufacturer offers different ways to use and configure these buttons, so you'll need to access your user guide to find out exactly how to do this.

1 Review the keys on the keyboard. Locate keys for volume, zoom, mail, Internet and similar options.

2 Press the key once to find out what happens.

3 If configurable, follow the directions to set the association.

ALERT: Most keyboards with configurable keys have an interface similar to the one shown here for configuring those keys.

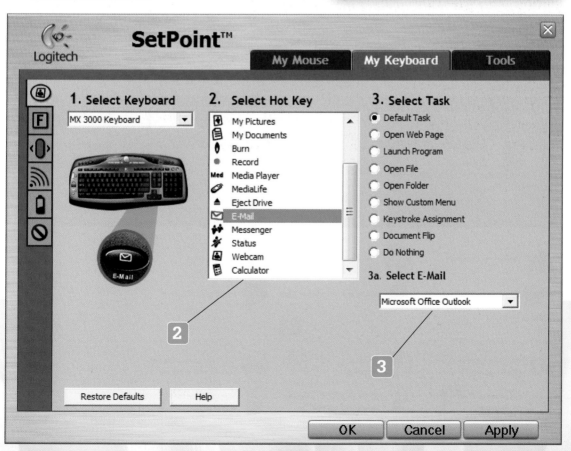

View the Welcome Center

When you first start Windows Vista, the Welcome Center opens. There are at least two sections: *Get started with Windows* and *Offers from Microsoft*, and perhaps some others not mentioned here. Often computer manufactures add their own listings and links to help you learn about your computer and the applications they've installed on it, as well as links to their own help files and website.

HOT TIP: From the Welcome Center you can view details about your computer, among other things.

DID YOU KNOW?
The Welcome Center can be found by typing Welcome in the Start search window, if it does not open automatically.

1 With the Welcome Center open, view the items under Get started with Windows.

2 Click What's new in Windows Vista.

3 If you do not want the Welcome Center to open every time you start Windows Vista, remove the check mark from Run at startup.

DID YOU KNOW?
When you click an item in the Welcome Center, the top of the page changes to reflect your choice.

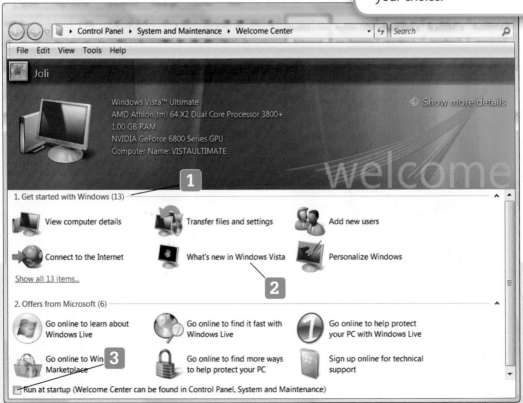

Watch demonstration videos

Windows Vista offers demonstration videos. You may be interested in watching the videos regarding the basics. These video demonstrations show you how to use the mouse, use the desktop, print, work with files, use the Web (Internet) and more.

1 Open the Welcome Center. Under Get started with Windows, click Show all ___ items...

2 Double-click Windows Vista Demos.

3 Click Watch the demo to watch it.

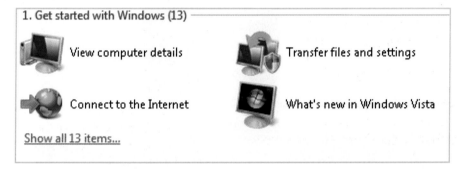

4 To stop the demo, or to close Windows Media Player, click the X in Windows Media Player.

WHAT DOES THIS MEAN?
Windows Media Player: A program that is included with Windows Vista for viewing videos, listening to music and viewing pictures.

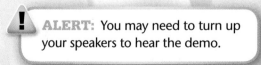

ALERT: You may need to turn up your speakers to hear the demo.

Shut down Windows safely

When you're ready to turn off your computer, you need to do so using the method detailed here. Simply pressing the power button can damage the computer or the operating system.

1 Click Start.

2 Click the arrow shown here.

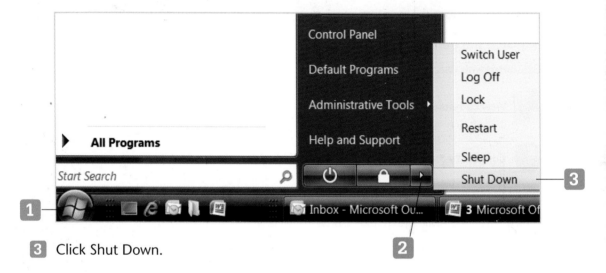

3 Click Shut Down.

2 Computing essentials

Introduction

To get the most out of your computer you need to understand some basic computing essentials. For example, it's important to understand what a window is, and how to resize, move and arrange open windows on your desktop. Each time you open a program, file, folder, picture or anything else on your computer, a new window almost always opens. You have to be very familiar with these windows, including how to show and hide them, in order to navigate your computer comfortably.

Beyond understanding windows, though, you'll need to know how to get help when you need it. Just about anything you could ask for can be found in the Help and Support Center in Vista. Finally, you have to know how to open an application, and how to search for an application when you can't find it.

ALERT: Read this chapter before reading any others. Throughout this book you'll be asked to work with windows and locate and open applications.

Use the Start button

Whenever you need to open an application or a personal folder, or access system tools, you'll use the Start button. Clicking the Start button opens the Start menu, where anything and everything is accessible.

1 Click the Start button. It's at the bottom of the screen.

2 Locate All Programs. Clicking All Programs opens a new menu, called the All Programs menu.

3 Locate your name in the Start menu. Clicking your name opens your personal folder.

4 Locate the folders for Documents, Pictures, Music and Games. Clicking any of these opens the folder.

5 Locate Control Panel. Control Panel is where you make changes to the computer defaults.

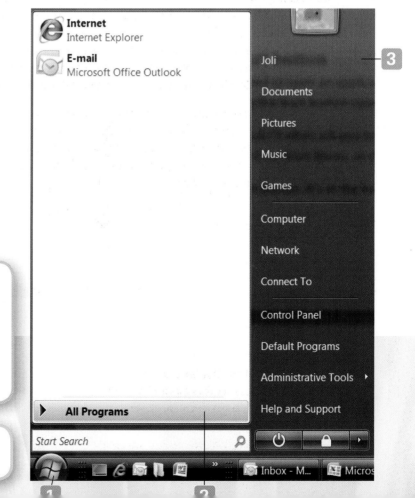

ALERT: In this book I'll often ask you to open a folder or application. You'll need to know how to use the Start button and the Start menu, so don't skip this section!

? DID YOU KNOW?
Folders open in windows.

Open your personal folder

You store the data you want to keep in your personal folder. Your data include documents, pictures, music, contacts, videos and more. The Start menu offers a place to easily access this folder, as well as installed programs, Vista features and applications (such as Windows Mail and Internet Explorer), recent items you've accessed and games, among other things.

1 Click Start.

2 Click your user name.

3 View the items in your personal folder.

? DID YOU KNOW?

You can click on anything you see in the Start menu to open it, and then close it using the X in the top right corner of the program window. Don't worry – you can't hurt anything by doing this.

🔥 HOT TIP: Double-click any folder inside your personal folder to open it. Click the back arrow to return to the previous view (also called a window).

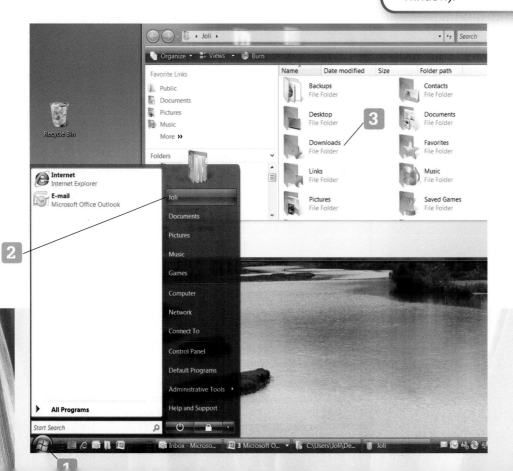

Close a folder or window

Each time you click an icon in the Start menu, in the All Programs menu or on the desktop, a window opens to display its contents. The window will stay open until you close it. To close a window, click the X in the top right corner of the window.

1 Click Start.

2 Click your user name. Your personal folder opens.

3 Click the X in the top right corner to close it.

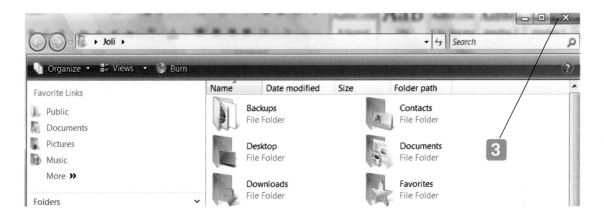

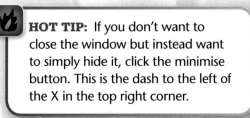

HOT TIP: If you don't want to close the window but instead want to simply hide it, click the minimise button. This is the dash to the left of the X in the top right corner.

Minimise a window

When you have several open windows, you may want to minimise (hide) the windows you aren't using. A minimised window appears on the taskbar as a small icon and is not on the desktop. When you're ready to use the window again, you simply click the relevant icon in your taskbar.

1 Open any window. (Click Start, and then click Pictures, Documents, Games or any other option.)

2 Click the – sign in the top right corner.

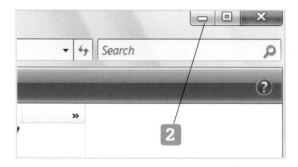

WHAT DOES THIS MEAN?

Taskbar: The grey bar that runs across the bottom of your screen. It contains the Start button icons for open programs and folders and additional information.

3 Locate the window title in the taskbar. Position your mouse over the icon to see its thumbnail.

ALERT: A minimised window is on the taskbar and is not shown on the desktop. You can restore the window by clicking on its icon on the taskbar. Restoring a window to the desktop brings the window back up so you can work with it.

ALERT: You won't see the thumbnail shown here unless you have Aero enabled. See Enable Aero in Chapter 3.

Restore a window

A window can be minimised (on the taskbar), maximised (filling the entire desktop) or in restore mode (not maximised or minimised, but showing on the desktop). When a window is in restore mode, you can resize or move the window as desired. You cannot resize or move windows that are minimised or maximised.

1 Open a window.

2 In the top right corner of the window, locate the two square buttons.

3 Click the button to put the window in restore mode.

ALERT: In order to put a window in restore mode, you have to have access to the restore button. The restore button is made up of two squares that appear next to the X in the top right corner of any window.

This window is already in restore mode

Click here to put this window in restore mode

ALERT: Remember: if you don't see two squares but instead see only one, the window is already in restore mode.

Maximise a window

A maximised window is as large as it can be and takes up the entire screen. You can maximise a window that is on the desktop by clicking the square icon in the top right corner. If the icon is already a square, the window is already maximised.

1 Open a window.

2 In the top right corner of the window, locate the square.

3 Click the square to maximise the window.

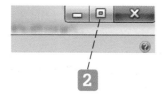

2

4 Once maximised you'll have the option to minimise, restore or close.

ALERT: Remember: if you see two squares instead of one, the window is already maximised.

Move a window

You can move a window as long as it's in restore mode. You move a window by dragging it from its title bar. The title bar is the bar that runs across the top of the window. Moving windows allows you to position multiple windows across the screen.

1. Open any window.

2. Put the window in restore mode if it is not already.

3. Left-click with the mouse on the title bar and drag. Let go of the mouse when the window is positioned correctly.

? DID YOU KNOW?

You can open a document or a picture and it will open in a window.

Resize a window

Resizing a window allows you to change the dimensions of the window. You can resize a window by dragging from its sides, corners, top or bottom.

1 Open any window. (If you're unsure, click Start and select Pictures.)

2 Put the window in restore mode. You want the maximise button to show.

3 Position the mouse at one of the window corners, so that the mouse pointer becomes a two-pointed arrow.

4 Hold down the mouse button and drag the arrow to resize the window.

5 Repeat as desired, dragging from the sides, top, bottom or corners.

ALERT: You can move and resize windows only if they are in restore mode, meaning that the maximise button is showing in the top right corner of the window.

Change the view in a window

When you open your personal folder from the Start menu, you will see additional folders inside it. These folders include Documents, Pictures and Music, among others. You'll use these subfolders to organise the data you create and save, such as documents, pictures and songs. You open a folder to see what's in it. You can change what the content inside these folders looks like. You can configure each folder independently so that the data appear in a list, as small icons and as large icons, to name just a few examples.

 HOT TIP: Show items in the Pictures folder as large or extra large icons, and you'll be able to tell what each picture looks like without actually opening it in a program.

1 Click Start.

2 Click Pictures.

3 Click the arrow next to Views.

4 Move the slider to select an option from the list.

HOT TIP: Show items in the Documents window as Details to see the name of each document as well as the date it was created.

Use Help and Support

Sometimes you need a little bit more than a book can give you. When that happens, you'll need to access Windows Vista's Help and Support feature. You can access Help and Support from the Start menu.

1 Click Start.

2 Click Help and Support.

3 Select any topic to read more about it.

4 To view demos, articles and tips, click Windows Help and How-to.

5 To get help from online sources, click Windows Online Help.

6 Click the X in the top right of the Help and Support Center to close it.

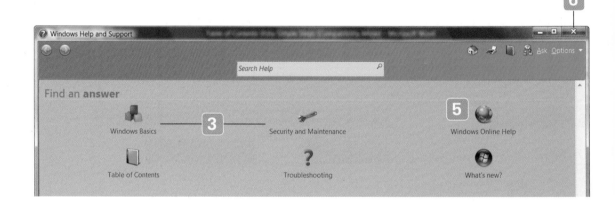

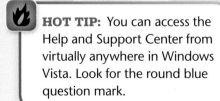

ALERT: If you click a topic, click the Back button in the top left corner of the Help and Support window to return to the previous screen.

HOT TIP: You can access the Help and Support Center from virtually anywhere in Windows Vista. Look for the round blue question mark.

Open an application

Programs (also called applications or software) offer computer users, like you, a way to perform tasks such as writing letters and editing photos. You open programs that are installed on your computer from the Start menu. Once a program is open, you can access its tools to perform tasks. For instance, if you open Windows Photo Gallery, you can use the interface options to view photos, fix problems with photos, place photos in categories, rate them and delete them, among other things.

1 Click Start.

2 Click All Programs.

3 If necessary, use the scroll bars to view all of the available applications.

4 Click any application to open it.

5 Click the X in the top right corner to close the application.

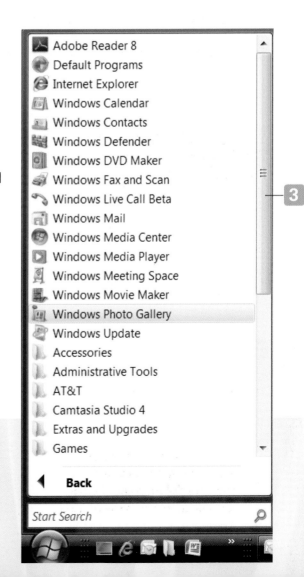

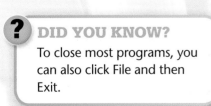

? DID YOU KNOW?
To close most programs, you can also click File and then Exit.

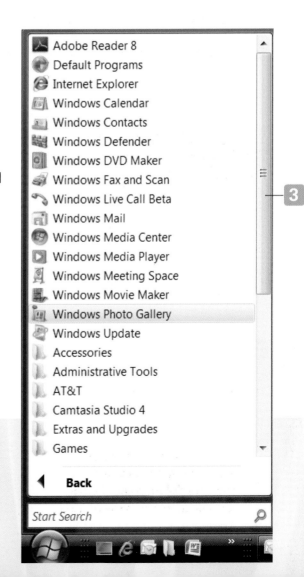

Adobe Reader 8
Default Programs
Internet Explorer
Windows Calendar
Windows Contacts
Windows Defender
Windows DVD Maker
Windows Fax and Scan
Windows Live Call Beta
Windows Mail
Windows Media Center
Windows Media Player
Windows Meeting Space
Windows Movie Maker
Windows Photo Gallery
Windows Update
Accessories
Administrative Tools
AT&T
Camtasia Studio 4
Extras and Upgrades
Games

◀ Back

Start Search

Search for a program with the Start menu

To locate a program on your computer you can search for it using the Start Search window. Just type in what you want, and select the appropriate program from the list. For instance, if you're looking for Windows Photo Gallery, and if you search for 'photo', you'll see much more than just Windows Photo Gallery in the results.

1 Click Start.

2 In the Start Search window, type 'photo'.

3 Note the results.

4 Click any result to open it. If you want to open Windows Photo Gallery, click it once. Note that it's under Programs.

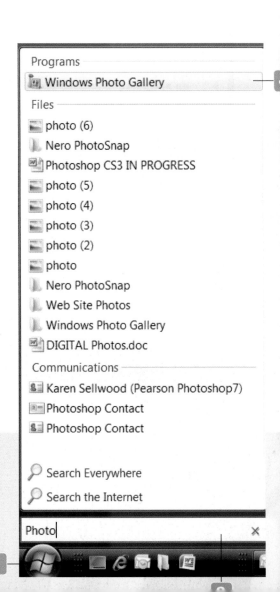

3 Vista essentials

Introduction

Vista comes with a lot of ways to personalise its interface. You can change the desktop background, apply a screen saver, add desktop icons and more. Vista also comes with something called the Sidebar, where you can add and configure gadgets that offer information in real time, such as the weather forecast. Some of these options require that you meet specific hardware requirements, so we'll start by looking at the details regarding your laptop.

View computer details

In order to apply some of the changes in this chapter, your laptop will have to meet some minimum requirements. For instance, you'll need to have at least 512 MB of RAM installed and you'll have to be running something other than Windows Basic, among other things. To see what is installed on your laptop, you'll use the Welcome Center.

HOT TIP: To open any application, click Start, and in the Start Search window type the name of the application to open. Click it under Programs in the results.

1 Open the Welcome Center.

2 Click View computer details. Read the information offered.

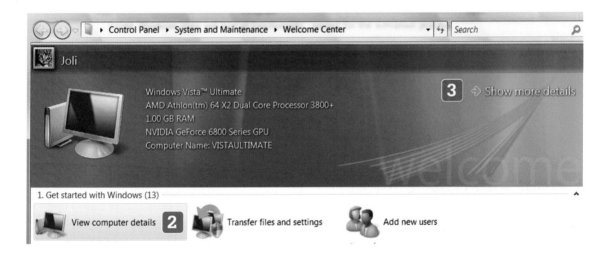

Joli

Windows Vista™ Ultimate
AMD Athlon(tm) 64 X2 Dual Core Processor 3800+
1.00 GB RAM
NVIDIA GeForce 6800 Series GPU
Computer Name: VISTAULTIMATE

3 ⇨ Show more details

1. Get started with Windows (13)

View computer details 2   Transfer files and settings   Add new users

3 Click Show more details.

4 Read the details regarding your computer.

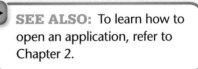

SEE ALSO: To learn how to open an application, refer to Chapter 2.

View basic information about your computer

Windows edition

Windows Vista™ Home Premium

Copyright © 2007 Microsoft Corporation. All rights reserved.

Service Pack 1
Upgrade Windows Vista

System

Manufacturer:	Acer
Model:	Aspire 5520
Rating:	3.0 Windows Experience Index
Processor:	AMD Turion(tm) 64 X2 Mobile Technology TL-58 1.90 GHz
Memory (RAM):	2.00 GB
System type:	32-bit Operating System

WHAT DOES THIS MEAN?

Processor: Short for microprocessor, the silicon chip that contains the central processing unit (CPU) inside a computer. Generally, the terms CPU and processor are used interchangeably. The CPU does almost all of the computer's calculations and is the most important piece of hardware in a computer system.

RAM: Short for random access memory, the hardware inside your computer that temporarily stores data that are being used by the operating system or programs. Although there are many types of RAM, all you need to know is that the more RAM you have, the faster your computer will (theoretically) run and perform.

GPU: Short for graphics processing unit, a processor used specifically for rendering graphics. Having a processor just for graphics frees up the main CPU, allowing the CPU to work faster on other tasks.

GHz: Short for gigahertz, a term that describes how fast a processor can work. One GHz equals one billion cycles per second, so a 2.4-GHz computer chip executes calculations at 240 billion cycles per second. Again, it's important to know only that the faster the chip, the faster the computer.

Change the screen saver

A screen saver is a picture or animation that covers your screen and appears after your computer has been idle for a specific amount of time that you set. For security, you can configure your screen saver to require a password on waking up, which happens when you move the mouse or hit a key on the keyboard. Requiring a password means that, once the screen saver is running, no one can log on to your computer, except you, by typing in your password when prompted.

1 Right-click an empty area of the desktop.

2 Click Personalize.

3 Click Screen Saver.

? DID YOU KNOW?
It used to be that screen savers saved your computer screen from image burn-in, but that is no longer the case.

> Screen Saver
>
> Change your screen saver or adjust when it displays. A screen saver is a picture or animation that covers your screen and appears when your computer is idle for a set period of time. — **3**

4 Click the arrow to see the available screen savers and select one.

5 Use the arrows to change how long to wait before the screen saver is enabled.

6 If desired, click On resume, display logon screen to require a password to log back into the computer.

7 Click OK.

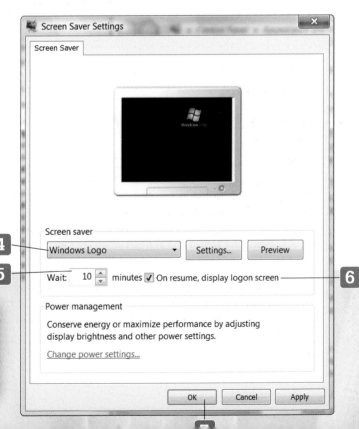

? DID YOU KNOW?
Select Photos and your screen saver will be a slideshow of photos stored in your Pictures folder.

Change the background

One of the first things you may want to do when you get a new PC or upgrade an older one is to personalise the picture on the desktop. That picture is called the background.

1 Right-click an empty area of the desktop.

2 Click Personalize.

3 Click Desktop Background.

4 For Location, select Windows Wallpapers. If it is not chosen already, click the down arrow to locate it.

5 Use the scroll bars to locate the wallpaper to use as your desktop background.

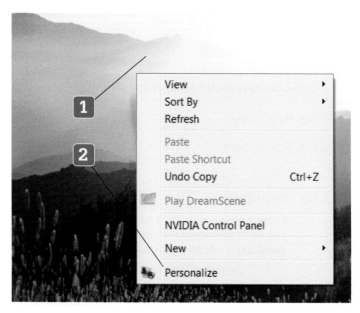

View	▶
Sort By	▶
Refresh	
Paste	
Paste Shortcut	
Undo Copy	Ctrl+Z
Play DreamScene	
NVIDIA Control Panel	
New	▶
Personalize	

Personalize appearance and sounds

 Window Color and Appearance
Fine tune the color and style of your windows.

 Desktop Background 3
Choose from available backgrounds or colors or use one of your own pictures to decorate the desktop.

 Screen Saver
Change your screen saver or adjust when it displays. A screen saver is a picture or animation that covers your screen and appears when your computer is idle for a set period of time.

? DID YOU KNOW?
You can click the Browse button to locate a picture you've taken, acquired or otherwise saved to your computer and then use it for a desktop background. Pictures are usually found in the Pictures folder.

6 Select a background to use.

7 Select a positioning option (the default is the most common).

8 Click OK.

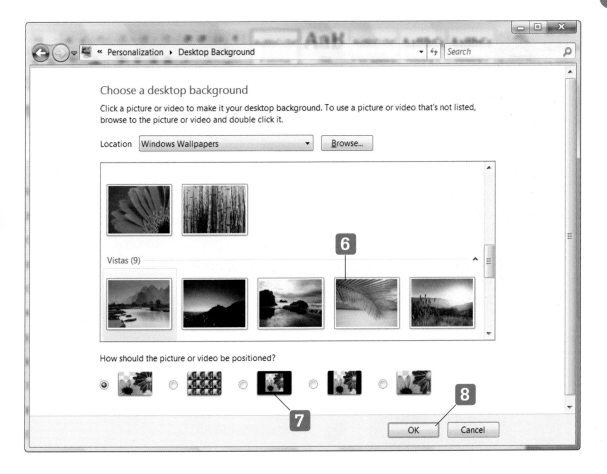

Add desktop icons

When you started Windows Vista for the first time, it may have had only one item on the desktop, the Recycle Bin. Alternatively, it may have had 20 or more. What appears on your desktop the first time Windows boots up depends on a number of factors, including who manufactured and installed the PC.

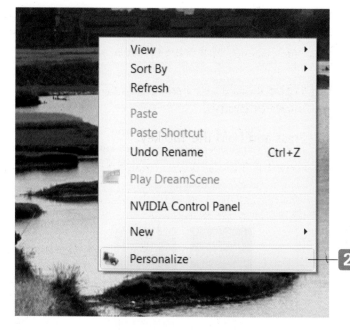

1 Right-click an empty area of the desktop.

2 Click Personalize.

3 Click Change desktop icons.

4 Select the desktop icons you want to appear on your desktop.

5 Click OK.

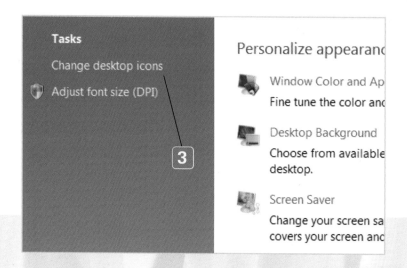

 HOT TIP: You can remove desktop icons by deselecting them here.

Use Flip

Windows Flip offers a quick way to choose a specific window when multiple windows are open. With Flip, you can scroll through open windows until you land on the one you want to use, and then select it.

1 With multiple windows open, on the keyboard hold down the Alt key with one finger or thumb.

2 Press and hold the Tab key.

3 Press the Tab key again, making sure that the Alt key is still depressed.

4 When the item you want to bring to the front is selected, let go of the Tab key and then let go of the Alt key.

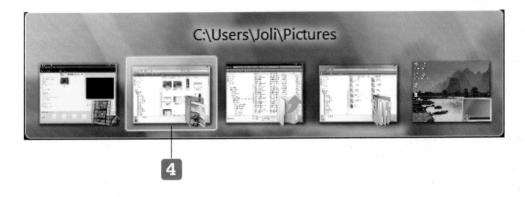

C:\Users\Joli\Pictures

4

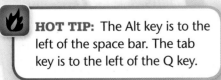

HOT TIP: The Alt key is to the left of the space bar. The tab key is to the left of the Q key.

Use Flip 3D

Windows Flip 3D offers a quick way to choose a specific window when multiple windows are open. With Flip 3D, you can scroll through open windows until you land on the one you want to use and then select it.

1 With multiple windows open, on the keyboard hold down the Windows key.

2 Click the Tab key once, while keeping the Windows key depressed.

3 Press the Tab key again, making sure that the Windows key is still depressed, to scroll through the open windows.

4 When the item you want to bring to the front is selected, let go of the Tab key and then let go of the Windows key.

 SEE ALSO: Locate specialised keyboard keys in Chapter 1.

 HOT TIP: The Windows key is the key to the left of the space bar and has the Windows logo printed on it.

 ALERT: If Flip 3D doesn't work, or if you get only Flip and not Flip 3D, either your PC does not support Aero or it is not configured to use it.

Enable the Sidebar

Windows Sidebar is a nifty feature that sits on your desktop and offers information on the weather and time and date, among other things. You can customise the Sidebar by hiding it, keeping it on top of or underneath open windows, adding or removing gadgets, and even detaching gadgets from the Sidebar for use anywhere on the desktop. Here you can see the parts of the Sidebar:

1 If the Sidebar is not on the desktop, click Start.

2 In the Start Search window, type Sidebar.

3 Under Programs, click Windows Sidebar.

? DID YOU KNOW?
By default, the Sidebar is enabled. If you can see the Sidebar, skip this section.

! ALERT: You won't get up-to-date information on the weather, time, and other real-time data unless you're connected to the Internet.

Enable Aero

Aero is an interface enhancement that you can enable for a cleaner, sleeker interface and Vista experience. You can use Aero only if your computer hardware supports it. Windows Aero builds on the basic Windows Vista interface and offers a high-performing desktop experience that includes, among other things, the translucent effect of Aero Glass.

1 Right-click an empty area of the desktop.

2 Click Personalize.

3 Click Windows Color and Appearance.

? DID YOU KNOW?
Aero Glass offers visual reflections and soft animations, making the interface quite comfortable.

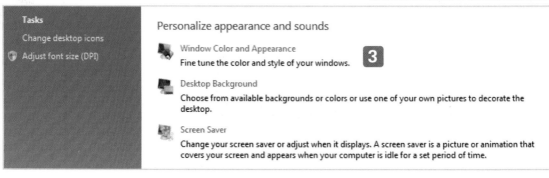

Tasks
Change desktop icons
Adjust font size (DPI)

Personalize appearance and sounds

Window Color and Appearance
Fine tune the color and style of your windows.   **3**

Desktop Background
Choose from available backgrounds or colors or use one of your own pictures to decorate the desktop.

Screen Saver
Change your screen saver or adjust when it displays. A screen saver is a picture or animation that covers your screen and appears when your computer is idle for a set period of time.

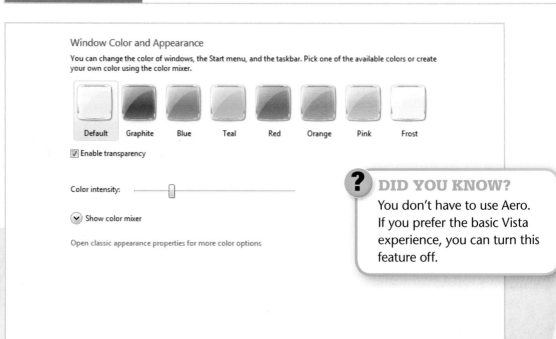

Window Color and Appearance
You can change the color of windows, the Start menu, and the taskbar. Pick one of the available colors or create your own color using the color mixer.

Default   Graphite   Blue   Teal   Red   Orange   Pink   Frost

☑ Enable transparency

Color intensity:

Show color mixer

Open classic appearance properties for more color options

? DID YOU KNOW?
You don't have to use Aero. If you prefer the basic Vista experience, you can turn this feature off.

OK   Cancel

4 If you're not using Aero already, you'll see the Appearance Settings dialogue box. If you're currently using Windows Aero, you'll see the Aero options, shown opposite.

5 To change from Windows Vista Basic to Windows Aero, click Windows Aero in the Colour Scheme options, and then click OK.

! ALERT: You don't have to do anything if Aero is already enabled.

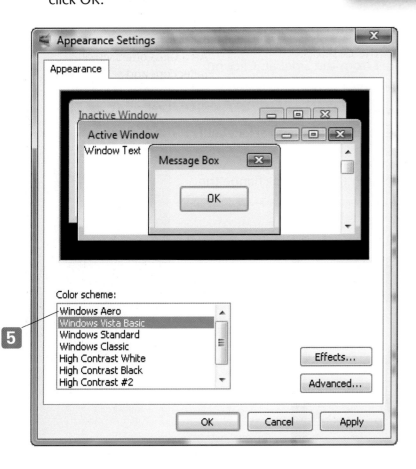

5

? DID YOU KNOW?
You can't use Flip 3D unless Aero is enabled.

Set the time on the clock gadget

Almost all gadgets on the Sidebar offer a wrench icon when you position your mouse over them. You can use this icon to access settings for the gadget. The first thing you may want to set is the time on the clock gadget.

1 Position the mouse pointer over the clock in the Sidebar. Look for the small X and the wrench to appear. Clicking the X will remove the gadget from the Sidebar. Clicking the wrench will open the gadget's properties, if properties are available.

2 Click the arrow in the Time zone window and select your time zone from the list.

3 Click the right arrow underneath the clock to change the clock type.

4 Click OK.

Clock

1 of 8 **3**

Clock name:

Time zone:

Current computer time

☐ Show the second hand **2**

Change computer date and time

OK   Cancel

4

SEE ALSO: The Sidebar must be enabled to access the clock icon. To enable the Sidebar, see page 57.

ALERT: The Stocks gadget runs about 15 minutes behind real-time stock data, so don't start buying and selling based on what you see here!

Add or remove a Sidebar gadget

Windows Vista comes with several gadgets in its Gadget Gallery, allowing you to add gadgets easily. You can remove gadgets from the Sidebar by clicking the X icon that appears when you hover the mouse over them.

1 To add a gadget, right-click an empty area of the Sidebar.

2 Click Add Gadgets.

3 In the Gadget Gallery, drag the gadget you want to add to the Sidebar and drop it there. Repeat as desired.

4 Click the X in the Gadget Gallery to close it.

5 Click the X in any gadget to remove it from the Sidebar. This does not remove it from the computer. Remember that the x will not appear until you hover the mouse over it.

? DID YOU KNOW?
Right-click an empty area of the Sidebar and select Properties to change what side of the desktop the Sidebar appears on.

! ALERT: Although you can get gadgets online, make sure you read the reviews of the gadgets you want before downloading and installing them: they could be buggy or dangerous. Don't be afraid to get gadgets online: just be careful and read the reviews before installing.

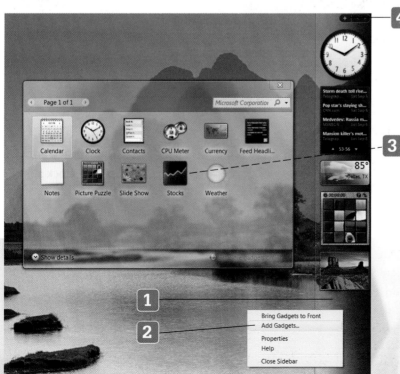

Close the Sidebar

Not everyone likes the Sidebar. If you want to close it, use a right-click.

1 Right-click an empty area of the Sidebar.

2 Click Close Sidebar.

Bring Gadgets to Front
Add Gadgets...

Properties
Help

Close Sidebar

? DID YOU KNOW?
You can show the Sidebar by clicking the Sidebar icon on the taskbar. The taskbar is the grey bar that runs across the bottom of your screen.

4 Mobility essentials

Introduction

Windows Mobility Center is available only on laptop computers and offers special features just for users who are on the go. No matter what kind of mobile computer you use, you've got easy access to power management options, wireless features, presentation capabilities, battery status and sync options.

Many of these features will prove quite useful. You'll find yourself selecting a power plan to improve battery life, using presentation settings when playing a slideshow, and turning off wireless capabilities when you're on an aeroplane, among other things.

Open the Mobility Center

Almost everything you'll need when unplugged and mobile can be found in the Mobility Center.

1 Click Start.

2 Type Mobility.

3 Under Programs, in the results, click Windows Mobility Center.

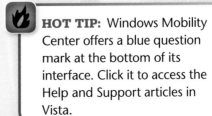

DID YOU KNOW?
Windows Mobility Center is available only on mobile PCs, such as laptops, notebooks, smart PCs and tablet PCs.

HOT TIP: Windows Mobility Center offers a blue question mark at the bottom of its interface. Click it to access the Help and Support articles in Vista.

Adjust screen brightness

When disconnected from a power source, you should reduce the brightness of the display to conserve battery power.

1 Open Mobility Center.

2 Move the brightness slider to the left to reduce the current brightness level.

? DID YOU KNOW?

Changing the brightness in Mobility Center will change the brightness only temporarily. It will not change the brightness as it is configured in Control Panel's Power Settings.

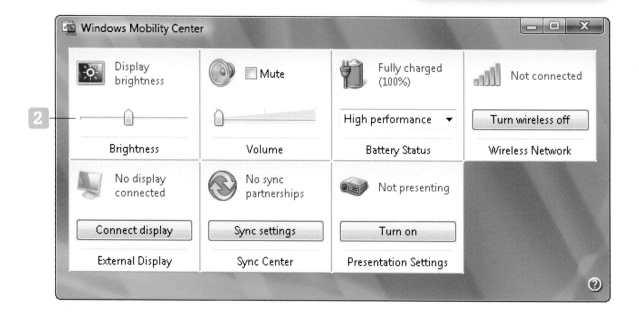

HOT TIP: Minimise the Mobility Center to keep it available on the taskbar.

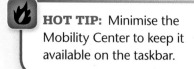

SEE ALSO: Minimising a window is covered in Chapter 2.

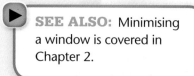

Change the volume

When on an aeroplane or in a meeting, for example, you may want to reduce the volume or mute it completely so as not to disturb others. You can change the volume on the taskbar or in the Mobility Center.

1 Open Mobility Center.

2 Move the volume slider to the left to reduce the volume.

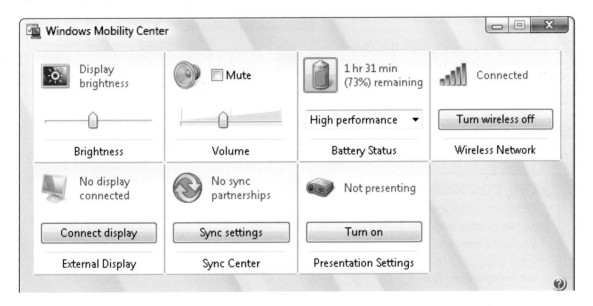

3 Click Mute to mute the volume completely.

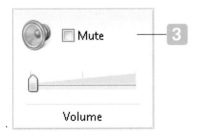

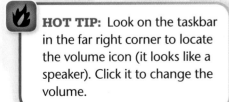

HOT TIP: Look on the taskbar in the far right corner to locate the volume icon (it looks like a speaker). Click it to change the volume.

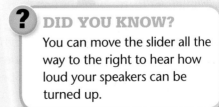

DID YOU KNOW?

You can move the slider all the way to the right to hear how loud your speakers can be turned up.

View battery life and change battery status

HOT TIP: The easiest way to conserve battery power and improve battery life is to use the Power saver plan, available in Windows Mobility Center, among other places.

From the Battery Status window in Windows Mobility Center, you can see how much life is left in your battery's current charge. You can change the power plan currently used here too.

1 Open Mobility Center.

2 Click the arrow to view the three power plans: Balanced, Power saver and High performance. Pick one.

3 View the current status of the battery life.

DID YOU KNOW?

There is a battery meter icon on the taskbar and it looks like a power meter and plug. To see the status of the battery, hover the mouse over it.

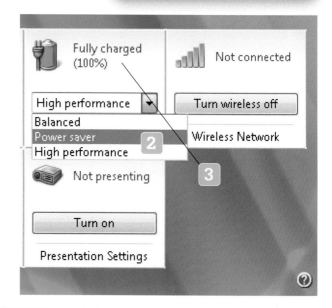

WHAT DOES THIS MEAN?

Balanced: This is the default power plan. You won't get the best power savings with this plan, and you won't get the best performance either. While the laptop is plugged into a power source, the display and hard disk are turned off after 20 minutes of inactivity; after 60 minutes of inactivity, the computer will go to sleep. When the laptop is running on battery power, Windows will turn off the display after 5 minutes and will turn off the hard drive after 10 minutes of inactivity. The PC will go to sleep after 15 minutes of inactivity while on battery power.

Power saver: This plan is all about lengthening battery life. That means in all instances, even when the laptop is plugged in, you'll notice decreased brightness and processor levels, and the computer will go to sleep, turn off hard disks, and turn off the display within minutes of inactivity.

High performance: This plan is all about enhancing performance. This power plan doesn't worry about battery life. Here, Vista provides 100 per cent of your CPU's processing power, which is necessary for playing games and performing resource-intensive tasks. The computer will still turn off its display, put the hard drive to sleep and put the computer to sleep after a set amount of idle time.

Turn on and off WiFi

You may want to turn off WiFi to increase battery life or if you are told to do so by an airline pilot before take-off.

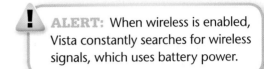
ALERT: When wireless is enabled, Vista constantly searches for wireless signals, which uses battery power.

1 Open Mobility Center.

2 Click Turn wireless off to disable WiFi.

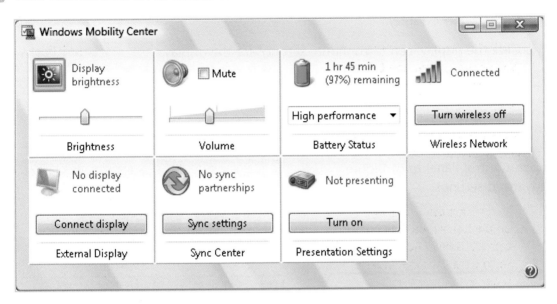

3 Click Turn wireless on to enable it.

? DID YOU KNOW?

With WiFi turned off you can still use your laptop on a plane, once you're instructed it's OK to use electronic devices.

? DID YOU KNOW?

Screen Rotation is an option you'll see only if you are using a tablet PC. Use it to change the orientation from portrait to landscape, and vice versa.

Connect to an external display

You can connect your laptop to an external display such as a projector, television or monitor when giving a presentation or working for long periods to enhance the visual display.

1 Connect and turn on the external display.

2 Open Mobility Center.

3 Click Connect display.

4 Click the display icon to configure settings for the display.

5 Make any desired changes to the display settings.

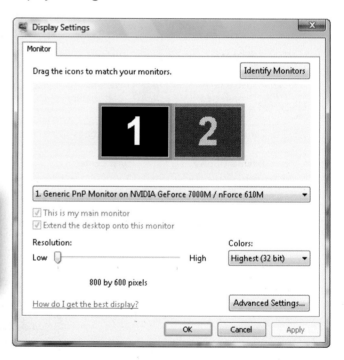

To select different settings, go to Display Settings in Control Panel and click Display Settings to open Control Panel to configure advanced settings.

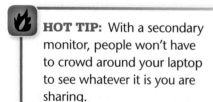

HOT TIP: With a secondary monitor, people won't have to crowd around your laptop to see whatever it is you are sharing.

WHAT DOES THIS MEAN?

Duplicate my desktop on all displays (mirrored): This option simply duplicates what you see on your laptop's display on the external display.

Show different parts of my desktop on each display (extended): This option will show what's on your laptop's single display across it and the external monitor. If you choose this, you must also select where the external display is connected, to the left or right of the laptop.

Show my desktop on the external display only: This will disable your laptop's monitor and show the display only on the external monitor (great for TV and DVD watching).

Turn on Presentation Settings

Vista's Mobility Center's Presentation Settings lets you disable your usual power management settings temporarily, to make certain that your system stays awake while you give a presentation.

1 Open Mobility Center.

2 Click Turn on in the Presentation Settings window (it will then change to Turn off).

3 Click the projector icon to configure the presentation settings.

4 Make configuration changes as desired.

5 Click OK.

WHAT DOES THIS MEAN?

There are presentation settings you can configure too. They include:

I am currently giving a presentation: Check this option to enable Presentation Settings.

Turn off the screen saver: Check this option to disable the screen saver.

Set the volume to: Use the slider to configure the volume.

Show this background: Check this to temporarily change the desktop background.

Connected displays: Click this to use an external display.

? DID YOU KNOW?

Presentation Settings lets you adjust what is necessary for giving a presentation. You can turn off the screen saver, change the volume and select a new desktop background image. You can also access alternative connected displays.

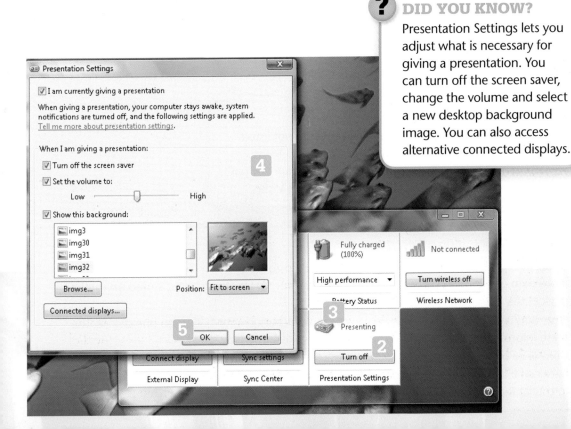

View the Sync Center

Sync Center can help you keep your files, music, contacts, pictures and other data in sync between your computer and mobile devices, network files and folders, and compatible programs such as Outlook.

ALERT: You need to use Sync Center only if you keep files in more than one location, such as a portable music player, back-up device, home computer or mobile phone.

1. Open Windows Mobility Center.

2. Click Sync settings.

3. The Sync Center opens. To set up a sync partnership, click Set up new sync partnerships and follow the directions given.

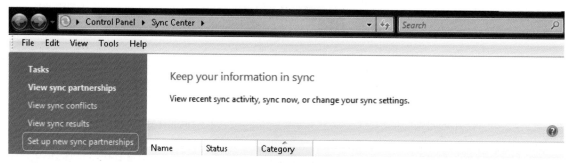

? DID YOU KNOW?

You might also see additional settings that are not listed here, supplied by your computer manufacturer. These settings will be specific to your mobile PC and are not part of the mobility settings included with Windows Vista.

WHAT DOES THIS MEAN?

Sync: The process of keeping files matched and up-to-date, when those files are used on more than one device. This prevents multiple versions of files from being stored on multiple devices.

One-way sync: In this type of sync, any time you change information on one device, the same information is changed on the second. It's like a one-way street.

Two-way sync: This type of sync is a two-way street. You might create a two-way sync between a laptop and a home or work computer. Changes made on the desktop PC will sync to the laptop, and vice versa.

Change when the computer sleeps

You can change how much time elapses before the computer goes to sleep. The less idle time configured, the more battery power you'll save.

 HOT TIP: To learn more about power plans, click Tell me more about power plans in the Power Options window.

1 Open Mobility Center.

2 In the Battery Status window, click the battery icon.

3 Click Change when the computer sleeps.

4 Edit the plan settings to the desired configuration and click Save changes.

Fully charged (100%)

High performance ▼

Battery Status

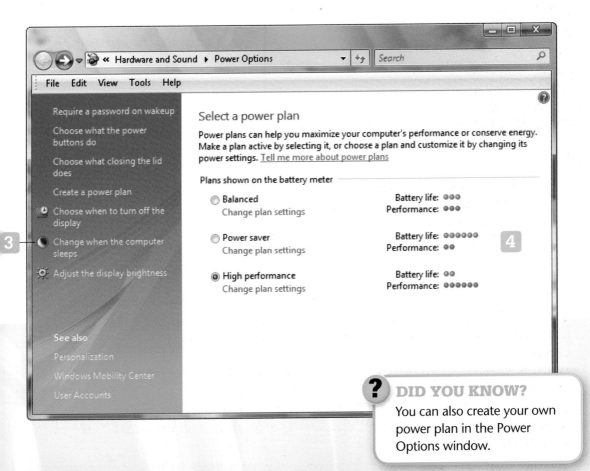

? **DID YOU KNOW?**

You can also create your own power plan in the Power Options window.

Change what happens when you press the power button or close the laptop's lid

You can change what happens when you press the power button or close the laptop's lid. You can choose from Shut down, Do nothing, Sleep and Hibernate.

1 Open Mobility Center.

2 In the Battery Status window, click the battery icon.

3 Click Choose what the power buttons do.

4 Edit the plan settings to the desired configuration and click Save changes.

DID YOU KNOW?

I use my laptop to record television shows in the middle of the night, so the laptop must remain on. However, I like to keep the lid closed. In this instance, I choose Do nothing for When I close the lid.

HOT TIP: If the laptop is plugged in, choose Sleep in instances when the laptop will be inactive for less than a day, and choose Hibernate when it's longer. Choose Shut down when you plan to move the laptop or when you won't be using it for a while.

Fully charged (100%)

High performance ▼

Battery Status

Define power buttons and turn on password protection

Choose the power settings that you want for your computer. The changes you make to the settings on this page apply to all of your power plans.

🛡 Change settings that are currently unavailable

Power and sleep buttons and lid settings

	On battery	Plugged in
When I press the power button:	Shut down	Shut down
When I press the sleep button:	Sleep	Sleep
When I close the lid:	Do nothing	Do nothing

Password protection on wakeup

◉ Require a password (recommended)
   When your computer wakes from sleep, no one can access your data without entering the correct password to unlock the computer. Create or change your user account password

○ Don't require a password
   When your computer wakes from sleep, anyone can access your data because the computer isn't locked.

Save changes   Cancel

Train a tablet PC

If you have a tablet PC you have the ability to write on it using a stylus. Once you've written something in your own handwriting, you can then tell Vista to convert your writing into regular text. Before you can do this though, you should spend some time training your tablet PC to recognise your handwriting.

1 Open the Tablet PC Input Panel.

2 Tap Tools with your stylus.

3 Tap Personalize Handwriting Recognition.

4 TapTeach the recogniser your handwriting style.

5 Work through as many screens as you have time for.

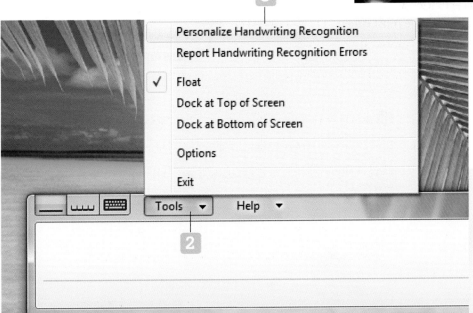

Connect to a free hotspot

If your laptop has wireless capabilities, you can connect to free WiFi hotspots. Doing so lets you access the Internet without physically connecting to a router or phone line, and without having to pay a monthly wireless bill.

1 Turn on your wireless laptop within range of a wireless network.

2 You'll be prompted from the Notification area that wireless networks are available.

ALERT: Often you'll have to go into the building that offers the wireless connection, or sit right outside, perhaps in a patio area.

3 Click Connect to a network.

ALERT: If you don't see a pop-up, click Start and click Connect To.

ALERT: Choose the wireless option with the most green bars.

ALERT: If prompted, choose Public network.

4 If more than one wireless network is available, locate the one that you want to use.

5 Click Connect.

! **ALERT:** WiFi must be enabled in the Mobility Center and Network Discovery must be enabled in the Network and Sharing Center for this to happen.

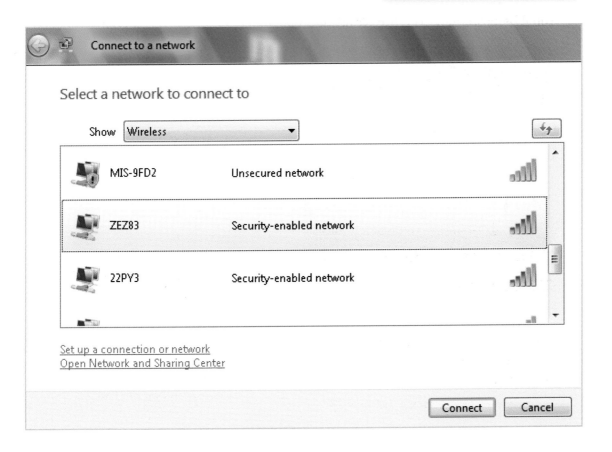

Connect to a network

Select a network to connect to

Show Wireless ▼

	MIS-9FD2	Unsecured network	
	ZEZ83	Security-enabled network	
	22PY3	Security-enabled network	

Set up a connection or network
Open Network and Sharing Center

Connect   Cancel

 HOT TIP: To find a WiFi hotspot close to you, go to **www.maps.google.com.uk** and search for WiFi hotspots. You'll find hotspots in many types of buildings including airports, hotels, bars, cafes, restaurants and more.

 SEE ALSO: For more on Enable network discovery, see Chapter 7. To learn how to turn on WiFi, see page 69.

5 Install hardware

Introduction

Your new laptop probably won't come with additional hardware such as a printer, DV camera or external speakers, although it may come with a built-in webcam or SD card reader. That said, you'll probably purchase or perhaps already own hardware that you'd like to use with your laptop. This *external* hardware must be connected and installed before you can use it.

In almost all instances, a hardware driver must be installed too. A driver is a piece of computer code that allows the device to communicate with Windows Vista, and vice versa. Drivers are different from the software you may also be prompted to install though so it's important to know the difference. In this chapter, you'll learn how to physically install printers, cameras and other hardware, and how to make them work with Windows Vista and your laptop.

Install a digital camera or webcam

If you have a laptop you may also have a digital camera. A digital camera is especially good if you take your laptop with you on holiday, because you can email pictures of your trip to friends and family back home. Before you can use the camera with your laptop, you have to install it.

1 Read the directions that come with the camera. If there are specific instructions for installing the driver, follow them. If not, continue here.

2 Plug the camera into a wall outlet, insert fresh batteries or install a freshly-charged battery pack as applicable.

3 Connect the camera to the PC using either a USB cable or a FireWire cable.

4 Insert the CD for the device, if you have it.

5 If a pop-up message appears, click the X to close the window. (The pop-up that may appear is not shown here.)

6 Turn on the camera. Place it in playback mode if that exists. Often, simply turning on the camera is enough.

7 Wait while the driver is installed.

> **! ALERT:** It's usually best to connect the new camera, turn it on and then let Vista install it. You need to intervene only if Vista can't install the hardware on its own.

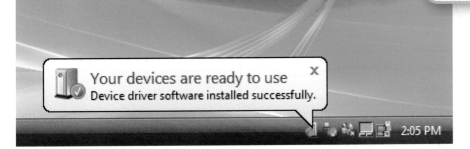

Your devices are ready to use ✕
Device driver software installed successfully.

2:05 PM

WHAT DOES THIS MEAN?

Driver: Software that allows the PC and the new hardware to communicate with each other.

USB: A technology used to connect hardware to a PC. A USB cable is often used to connect a digital camera to a PC.

FireWire: A technology used to connect hardware to a PC. A FireWire cable is a cable often used to connect a digital video camera to a PC.

Install a printer

If your laptop is your main computer, you will probably want to install a printer.

1 Connect the printer to a wall outlet.

2 Connect the printer to the PC using either a USB cable or a parallel port cable.

3 Insert the CD for the device, if you have it.

4 If a pop-up message appears regarding the CD, click the X to close the window.

5 Turn on the device.

6 Wait while the driver is installed.

Installing device driver software ✕
Click here for status.

2:03 PM

Install other hardware

To install other types of hardware, insert a driver CD if one came with the hardware, plug in the new hardware and turn it on, and wait for Windows Vista to install the required driver.

1 Connect the hardware to a PC and a wall outlet.

2 Insert the CD for the device, if you have it.

3 If a pop-up message appears regarding the CD, click the X to close the window.

4 Turn on the device.

5 Wait while the driver is installed.

ALERT: Occasionally, hardware manufacturers require you to install software first, then plug in the device, and then turn on the hardware. Read the instructions that come with your hardware to see what order to do things in.

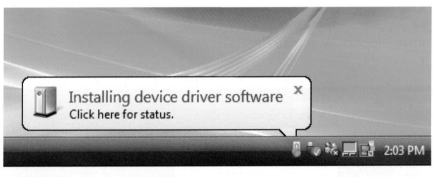

ALERT: When the instructions for a hardware device tell you to install the CD before connecting the hardware, it's often just a ruse to get you to install unnecessary software, so be aware of what you're installing.

ALERT: If the hardware does not install properly, refer to the user manual.

Locate a driver

As noted, most of the time, hardware installs automatically and with no input from you, other than plugging it in and turning it on. However, in rare cases, the hardware does not install properly or is simply not available. If you cannot replace the device with something that Vista recognises, you'll have to locate and install the driver yourself.

1 Write down the name and model number of the device.

2 Click Start, and click Internet Explorer.

3 Locate the manufacturer's website. If you find the manufacturer's website, skip to step 5.

4 If you can't find the manufacturer's website, search for it.

5 Locate a link for Support, Support and Drivers, Customer Support, or something similar. Click it.

 HOT TIP: It's best to refrain from installing hardware that does not have a signed driver.

 HOT TIP: The make and model of a device are usually written on the bottom of the device.

 Buy online or Call 800-BUY-MYHP

⌂ | **Shop for Products & Services**   **Support & Drivers**   **Explore & Create**

6 Locate your device by make, model or other characteristics.

 ALERT: Locating a driver is the first step. You must now download the driver and then install it.

WHAT DOES THIS MEAN?

Search: To type a name in a website's search window in order to find something on the Internet.

Signed driver: A driver is signed when Microsoft has fully tested the driver for functionality.

Unsigned driver: A driver is unsigned if it has not passed Microsoft's testing process to prove it works and won't cause problems for the computer.

 SEE ALSO: To open a website in Internet Explorer, see Chapter 7.

Download and install a driver

If you've located the driver you need, you can now download and install it. Downloading is the process of saving the driver to your computer's hard drive. Once you've downloaded the driver, you can install it.

1 Locate the driver as detailed in the previous section.

2 Click Download Driver, Obtain Software or something similar.

Driver

Description	Current version	Size (MB)	Estimated download time	Previous version	
HP LaserJet and Color LaserJet products - products supported and drivers included in Microsoft Windows Vista	N/A 6 Dec 2006	-	-	-	» Obtain software

3 Click Save.

4 Click Run, Install or Open Window to begin the installation.

5 Follow the directions in the set-up process to complete the installation.

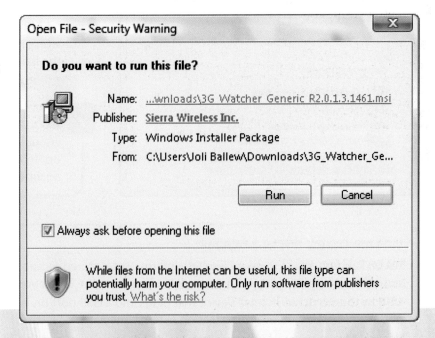

Open File - Security Warning

Do you want to run this file?

Name: ...wnloads\3G Watcher Generic R2.0.1.3.1461.msi
Publisher: Sierra Wireless Inc.
Type: Windows Installer Package
From: C:\Users\Joli Ballew\Downloads\3G_Watcher_Ge...

[Run]   [Cancel]

☑ Always ask before opening this file

⚠ While files from the Internet can be useful, this file type can potentially harm your computer. Only run software from publishers you trust. What's the risk?

 HOT TIP: Save the file in a location you recognise, such as Downloads.

 ALERT: If installation does not begin automatically, browse to the location of the file and double-click it to begin the installation manually.

Use ReadyBoost

ReadyBoost is a new technology that lets you add more RAM (random access memory) to your laptop easily, without opening the laptop case. Adding RAM often improves performance dramatically. ReadyBoost lets you use a USB flash drive or a secure digital memory card (like the one in your digital camera) as RAM, if it meets certain requirements.

1 Insert a USB flash drive, thumb drive, portable music player or memory card into an available slot on the outside of your laptop.

2 Wait while Windows Vista checks to see whether the device can perform as memory.

3 If prompted to use the flash drive or memory card to improve system performance, click Speed up my system.

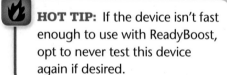 **ALERT:** USB keys must be at least USB 2.0 and have at least 64 MB of free space, but don't worry about that: you'll be told if the hardware isn't up to par.

HOT TIP: If the device isn't fast enough to use with ReadyBoost, opt to never test this device again if desired.

WHAT DOES THIS MEAN?

RAM: Random access memory is where information is stored temporarily so the operating system has quick access to it. The more RAM you have, the better your PC should perform.

USB or thumb drive: A small device that plugs into a USB port on your PC, often for the purpose of backing up or storing files on external media.

Portable music player: Often a small USB drive. This device also has a headphone jack and controls for listening to music stored on it.

Media card: A removable card used in digital cameras to store and transfer data to the PC.

Install software

As with installing hardware, software installation should go smoothly almost every time. Just make sure you get your software from a reliable source, such as Amazon, Microsoft's website, Apple's website or a decent high-street shop. Downloading software from the Internet is risky, and you never know whether it will run properly or contain adware or spyware.

1 Insert the CD or DVD in the appropriate drive.

2 If prompted, choose Run.

3 If you are not prompted:
   a. Click Start.
   b. Click Computer.
   c. Right-click the CD or DVD drive.
   d. Click Install or run program.

4 If prompted to cancel or allow, click Allow.

5 Work through the installation wizard.

HOT TIP: It's best to simply stay away from downloaded software unless the company is well known, such as Adobe, and you're willing to burn your own software back-up disks.

HOT TIP: Installing software requires you to put in the CD or DVD and follow the prompts.

ALERT: If you aren't prompted to install the software, click Start and then Computer, and then manually start the installation.

6 Pictures, music and media

Introduction

Windows Photo Gallery is included in all editions of Windows Vista and lets you easily upload, view, store, manage, access and edit your digital photos. Windows Media Player offers all you need to manage your music library, get music online, and copy the CDs from your own music collection to your laptop. You can also use it to burn music CDs that you can listen to in your car, watch DVDs, and more. Windows Media Center is a one-stop media application that lets you access and manage pictures, videos, movies, music, online media, television, DVDs, CDs and radio. Media Center really stands out for watching cable and Internet TV, online media and DVDs.

Upload digital photos

After you've taken pictures with your digital camera, you may want to move or copy those pictures to the laptop. Once stored on the laptop's hard drive, you can view, edit, email and print the pictures.

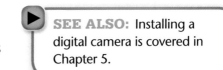 **SEE ALSO:** Installing a digital camera is covered in Chapter 5.

1 Connect the device. If applicable, turn it on.

2 When prompted, choose Import Pictures using Windows.

DID YOU KNOW?

These steps also work for importing pictures from a mobile phone.

3 Type a descriptive name for the group of pictures you're importing.

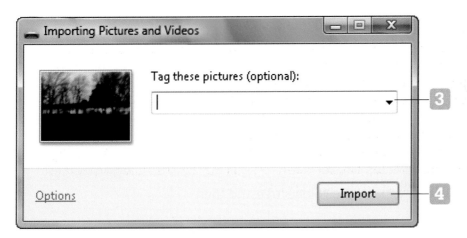

Importing Pictures and Videos

Tag these pictures (optional): —— 3

Options   Import —— 4

4 Click Import.

HOT TIP: If desired, check Erase after importing. This will cause Vista to erase the images from the device after the import is complete.

ALERT: If your device isn't recognised when you plug it in and turn it on, in Windows Photo Gallery click File, and then click Import from Camera or Scanner.

Open Photo Gallery and view a picture

You can use pictures in a lot of different ways with Vista, but Windows Photo Gallery is the best. With it, you have easy access to slideshows, editing tools and picture groupings. You can sort, filter and organise as desired.

1 Click Start.

2 Type Photo Gallery in the Start Search window.

3 From the Start results, under Programs, click Windows Photo Gallery.

? DID YOU KNOW?
You can click Start, and then All Programs, and then Windows Photo Gallery.

4 In the View pane, expand the Folders tree and then the Pictures tree.

WHAT DOES THIS MEAN?

View pane: The pane to the left is the View pane, where you select the folder or subfolder that contains the pictures you want to view, manage, edit or share.

Expand a tree: To click the right-facing arrow to show the contents of a folder.

Thumbnail pane: The pane on the right, where you preview the pictures in the folder selected in the View pane.

? DID YOU KNOW?
Your digital pictures are stored in the Pictures folder on your hard drive, not 'in' or 'by' Photo Gallery. Photo Gallery offers a place to view and work with images and has nothing to do with how they are stored on the PC.

Programs

📇 Windows Live Photo Gallery B

🖼 Windows Photo Gallery — **3**

🔍 Search Everywhere

🔍 Search the Internet

Photo Gallery — **2**

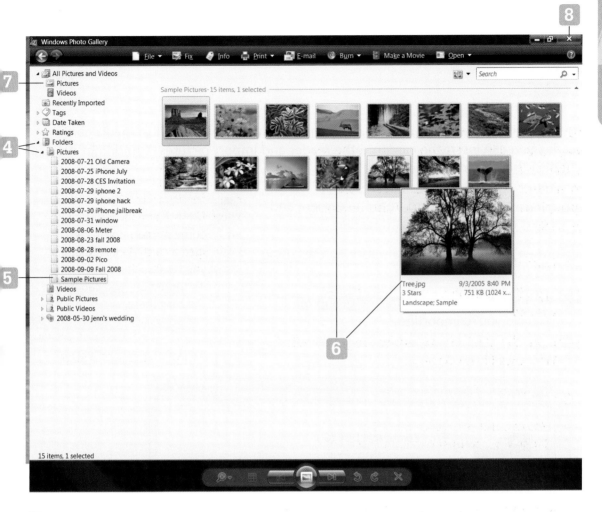

5 Select any folder name.

6 Hover the mouse over any picture to see a larger thumbnail of it.

7 Click Pictures at the top of the View window.

8 Click the X to close Windows Photo Gallery.

Import pictures from a media card

If your digital camera has a media card, and your laptop has a built-in media card reader, you can insert the card into the reader and import pictures. You do not have to connect the camera or turn it on.

1 Remove the media card from the camera and insert it into the media card reader.

2 When prompted, choose Import Pictures using Windows.

3 Type a descriptive name for the group of pictures you're importing.

4 Click Import.

? DID YOU KNOW?

Some printers come with media card readers built in. If you have such a printer, and it's turned on, you can insert the card there.

WHAT DOES THIS MEAN?

Media card: A small card about the size of your thumbnail that holds data in digital devices such as cameras.

Media card reader: A slot usually in the side of a laptop or on the front of a PC or printer that allows you to insert a media card and retrieve the information on it.

View a slideshow of pictures

To view pictures in a folder in full screen and have them move from one to the other automatically, view a slideshow of the pictures.

1 Open Windows Photo Gallery.

2 Expand any folder that contains pictures.

3 Click the Play Slide Show button. Wait at least three seconds.

4 To end the show, press the Esc key on the keyboard.

HOT TIP: Press the F11 key on the keyboard to start a slideshow.

Auto adjust picture quality

With pictures now on your laptop and available in Windows Photo Gallery, you can perform some editing. Photo Gallery offers the ability to correct brightness, contrast, tint and saturation, and other things.

1 Open Photo Gallery.

2 Double-click a picture to edit.

3 Click Fix.

4 Click Auto Adjust.

5 If you do not like the result, click File and click Undo.

6 Click Adjust Exposure.

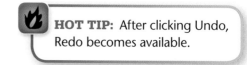

HOT TIP: After clicking Undo, Redo becomes available.

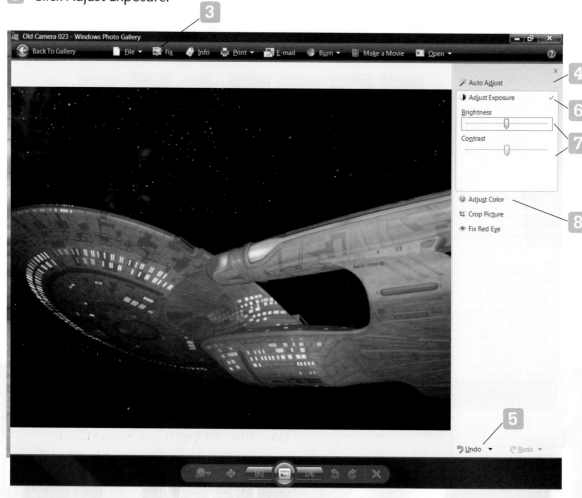

7 Move the sliders for Brightness and Contrast. Click Revert to return to the original image settings.

8 Click Adjust Color.

9 Move the sliders for Color Temperature, Tint and Saturation. Click Revert to return to the original image settings.

HOT TIP: To save changes, click File and then click Make a Copy.

ALERT: Click Back to Gallery to return to the picture gallery (the previous screen).

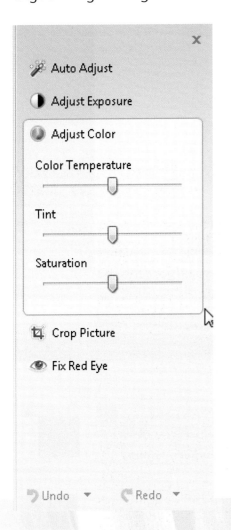

WHAT DOES THIS MEAN?

Auto Adjust: This tool automatically assesses and alters the image, which most of the time results in a better image. However, there's always the Undo button, and you'll likely use it on occasion.

Adjust Exposure: This tool offers slider controls for brightness and contrast. You move these sliders to the left and right to adjust as desired.

Adjust Color: This tool offers slider controls to adjust the temperature, tint and saturation of the photo. Temperature runs from blue to yellow, allowing you to change the atmosphere of the image. Tint runs from green to red, and saturation moves from black and white to colour.

Open Media Player

You open Media Player in the same way that you open other programs, from the Start menu. Once opened, you'll need to know where the Category button is, so you can access different kinds of media. We'll start with music.

1 Click Start.

2 Type Media Player.

3 Under Programs, click Media Player to open it.

4 Click the arrow next to the Category button.

5 Click Music.

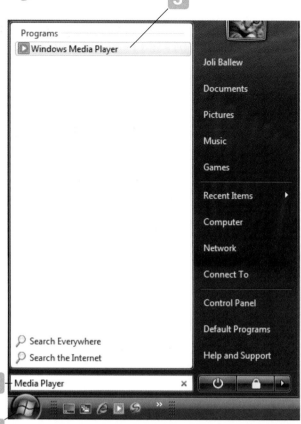

> **WHAT DOES THIS MEAN?**
>
> **Windows Media Player:** An application included with every Windows Vista edition. You can watch DVDs and videos here if you have Windows Vista Basic or Vista Business. If you have Vista Home Premium or Ultimate, you'll probably opt to watch DVDs in Media Center, because it's a more comprehensive media application.
>
> **Alert:** The first time you start Windows Media Player 11, you'll be prompted to set it up. Choose Express to accept the default settings.

> **? DID YOU KNOW?**
> By default, Music is selected.

> **? DID YOU KNOW?**
> You can select Pictures, Video or other options to access that type of media.

Listen to a song

▶ **SEE ALSO:** The previous section, Open Media Player.

To play any music track, simply navigate to it and double-click it. Songs are listed in the Navigation pane.

1 Open Media Player.

2 If necessary, click the Category button and choose Music.

3 Click Album. (Note you can also click Songs, Artists or any other category to locate a song.)

4 Double-click any album to play it.

? DID YOU KNOW?

The controls at the bottom of the screen, from left to right, are: Shuffle (to play songs in random order), Repeat, Stop, Previous, Play/Pause, Next, Mute and a volume slider.

? DID YOU KNOW?

Media Player has Back and Forward buttons that you can use to navigate Media Player.

Copy music files to a CD

There are two ways to take music with you when you are on the move. You can copy the music to your laptop or a portable device such as a music player, or you can create your own CDs, choosing the songs to copy and placing them on the CD in the desired order.

? **DID YOU KNOW?**
CDs that you create in Media Player can be played in car stereos and portable CD players, as well as lots of other CD devices.

1 Open Media Player.

2 Click the arrow under the Burn tab.

! **ALERT:** A typical CD can hold about 80 minutes of music.

? **DID YOU KNOW?**
Media Player will keep track of the songs you select and will let you know when you're running out of space on the CD you are creating.

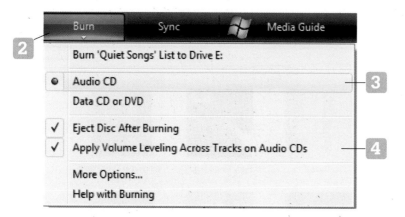

3 Verify that Audio CD has a dot by it. If it does not, click it once.

4 Verify that Apply Volume Leveling Across Tracks on Audio CDs has a check by it.

WHAT DOES THIS MEAN?
Burn: A term used to describe the process of copying music from a computer to a CD.
Volume leveling: Makes all songs on the CD record at the same volume, so that some tracks are not louder or softer than others.

5 Click outside the drop-down list to close it.

6 Insert a blank CD in the CD drive. (Close any pop-up dialogue boxes.)

7 Under Library, click Songs or Albums.

8 Click any song title or album that you want to add, and drag it to the List pane.

? **DID YOU KNOW?**
Look at the slider in the List pane to see how much room is left on the CD.

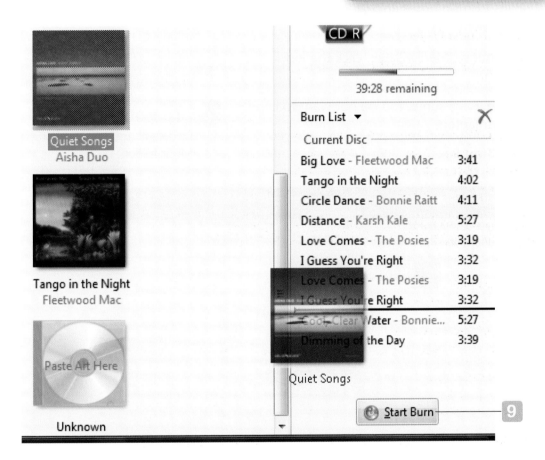

39:28 remaining

Burn List ▼   ✕

Current Disc ——————————————

Big Love - Fleetwood Mac	3:41
Tango in the Night	4:02
Circle Dance - Bonnie Raitt	4:11
Distance - Karsh Kale	5:27
Love Comes - The Posies	3:19
I Guess You're Right	3:32
Love Comes - The Posies	3:19
I Guess You're Right	3:32
Cool Clear Water - Bonnie...	5:27
Dimming of the Day	3:39

Quiet Songs

🔘 Start Burn —————— 9

Quiet Songs
Aisha Duo

Tango in the Night
Fleetwood Mac

Paste Art Here

Unknown

9 When you've added the songs you want, click Start Burn.

? **DID YOU KNOW?**
You can right-click any entry to access additional options, including Remove from List, Move Up and Move Down.

Copy a CD to your hard drive

You can copy CDs to your hard drive. This is called 'ripping'. To rip means to copy in media-speak. Once music is on your laptop, you can listen to it in Media Player, burn compilations of music to other CDs and put the music on a portable music player.

1 Insert the CD to copy into the CD drive.

2 If any pop-up boxes appear, click the X to close them.

3 In Windows Media Player, click the Rip button.

4 Deselect any songs you do not want to copy to your laptop.

5 Click Start Rip.

ALERT: When you insert a blank recordable CD, you may see pop-up boxes. Close them to rip a CD using the Windows Media Player interface.

DID YOU KNOW?
By default, music is saved in your Music folder.

HOT TIP: You can watch the rip progress in the List pane.

DID YOU KNOW?
The ripped music will now appear under Library and under Recently Added, as well as in Artist, Album, Songs, Genre and Year.

Watch a DVD

You can watch a DVD on your laptop just as you would on any DVD player. Vista offers two choices for doing so: Windows Media Center and Windows Media Player. We'll talk about Windows Media Player here.

1 Find the button on the laptop that opens the DVD drive door. Press it.

2 Place the DVD in the door and press the button again to close it.

3 When prompted, choose Play DVD movie using Windows Media Player.

? DID YOU KNOW?

If you have Windows Vista Home Premium or Vista Ultimate, you have Windows Media Center. It's best to watch DVDs in Media Center if you have it, rather than in Media Player.

SEE ALSO: If the DVD plays automatically and no choice is offered, refer to Change AutoPlay settings in Chapter 10.

 HOT TIP: The controls you see and use in Media Player are very similar to the controls on your own DVD player.

Open Media Center

You open Media Center in the same way that you open other programs, from the Start menu.

1 Click Start.

2 Click All Programs.

3 Click Windows Media Center.

HOT TIP: Media Center's interface includes several menus: TV + Movies, Sports, Online Media, Tasks, Pictures + Videos, and Music.

Set up Media Center

The first time you open Media Center, you'll be prompted to set it up. You'll need to configure several things: Internet connection, TV signal, speakers, and your TV or monitor. You may also see the option to join a wireless network.

ALERT: It's nearly impossible to detail here how to set up Media Center because of the sheer number of options. A generic introduction is offered, however.

1 Open Media Center.

2 When you see the Set Up screen shown here, start at the top and work your way down.

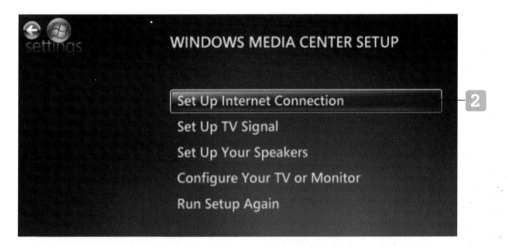

WINDOWS MEDIA CENTER SETUP

settings

Set Up Internet Connection — 2

Set Up TV Signal

Set Up Your Speakers

Configure Your TV or Monitor

Run Setup Again

? DID YOU KNOW?
Set Up walks you through each process, giving you options, pictures and diagrams to help you make the correct choices.

ALERT: Although some set-up options are not required, it's best to work through all of the options.

ALERT: You can't watch TV without a TV tuner!

Watch, pause and rewind live TV

When you open Media Center, TV + Movies is the default option, and Recorded TV is selected. To watch live television, you'll need to use the mouse or remote control to move to the right of recorded TV to live TV. While watching live TV, you can watch, pause and rewind the programme you're watching, and fast-forward through previously paused programming.

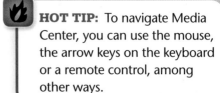

ALERT: If you receive an error when you click live TV, either you do not have the television signal properly set up or you don't have a TV tuner.

HOT TIP: To navigate Media Center, you can use the mouse, the arrow keys on the keyboard or a remote control, among other ways.

1 Open Media Center.

2 Move to the right of recorded TV one time and click live tv.

3 Position the mouse at the bottom of the live TV screen to show the controls.

4 Use the controls to manage live TV.

107

 HOT TIP: Press pause at the beginning of a 30-minute show for 10 minutes and you can fast-forward through the commercials. (For a 60-minute show, pause for 20 minutes.)

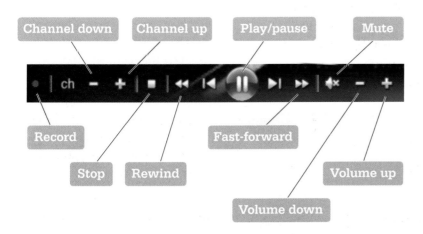

Channel down   Channel up   Play/pause   Mute

Record   Stop   Rewind   Fast-forward   Volume down   Volume up

WHAT DOES THIS MEAN?

Recorded TV: Click to access TV shows that you've recorded.

Live TV and/or Internet TV: View live or Internet TV.

Guide: View the Guide, which offers a list of scheduled TV programming, and use it to record a show or series.

Movies Guide: View movies.

Play DVD: Watch a DVD.

Search: Search for media by title, keyword, category, actor or director.

Obtain programme information

When you're watching live TV, you'll see the broadcast, but other items will also appear and disappear, based on where you move the mouse. The show's broadcast information appears when you change to the channel, and you can also bring it up by right-clicking an area of the screen.

1 Open Media Center.

2 Under TV + Movies, click live TV.

3 Right-click anywhere on the screen to access additional information about the show.

? DID YOU KNOW?

You can click any items in the list to open a new dialogue box that contains additional choices.

4 Click outside the list to remove it from the screen.

WHAT DOES THIS MEAN?

Program Info: Displays the Program Info screen, where you can record a single programme or a series, and acquire information about the show.

Record: Immediately starts recording the current television show.

Record Series: Immediately starts recording the current television show and schedules the television series to be recorded.

Zoom: Changes how the picture is displayed.

Mini Guide: Shows information about the show on the screen in a minimised format (compared with Program Info).

Settings: Opens Media Center Settings.

View your pictures

Although you can use Windows Photo Gallery to view your pictures, you may find you like Media Center better.

1 Open Media Center.

2 Scroll to Pictures + Videos, and click picture library.

3 Browse through the available pictures and picture folders.

4 Click play slide show to play a slideshow of the pictures in that folder.

HOT TIP: Position the mouse at the bottom of the screen to show the controls.

WHAT DOES THIS MEAN?

More Pictures: Access pictures from the Internet.

Picture Library: View the images on your computer, including those on a CD or DVD, and shared pictures on the network.

Play All: View a slideshow of the pictures on your PC.

Video Library: Access videos stored on the PC or network drives.

Watch a DVD

You know you can watch a DVD in Media Player, but you can also watch a DVD in Media Center.

1 Put a DVD in the DVD drive.

2 If prompted, choose Play DVD movie using Windows Media Center.

3 Use the mouse, remote control or arrows on the keyboard to play the movie, view special features and select other options.

4 Use the controls introduced earlier to pause, stop, rewind and fast-forward through the movie.

? DID YOU KNOW?

You can also browse to TV + Movies in Media Center, and from the submenus choose play dvd.

Listen to music

You know you can listen to music in Media Player, but you can also listen to music in Media Center.

1 Open Media Center.

2 Scroll to Music and click music library.

3 Locate the album that you want to play.

? DID YOU KNOW?

You can click artists, genres, songs, playlists and more to refine the list.

4 Click Play Album, or select any other option.

WHAT DOES THIS MEAN?

More Music: Access music on the Internet.

Music Library: Access your music and playlists created in Media Player 11, or search for music by various criteria.

Play All: Play the music in your music library, change the order in which songs are played, play visualisations, shuffle music, repeat songs and buy music.

Radio: Access local radio stations and configure presets.

Search: Search for the music you want.

7 Getting online and surfing the Internet

Introduction

Having a laptop often makes it extremely easy to get online. For instance, if you have the right hardware, you can simply get within range of a free WiFi hotspot and connect directly to the Internet at no cost at all (see Chapter 4). However, if you want to get online from anywhere and at any time, you'll need to do a few more things. You'll need to select an Internet service provider (ISP), subscribe to it, select a user name, password and email address, and obtain the required configuration settings.

Select an ISP

There are a tremendous number of options for connecting to the Internet. You can connect using your phone line (dial-up), using an existing cable connection (broadband or DSL) or wirelessly (satellite). You can also use a connection from a mobile phone provider, such as T-Mobile, which is often referred to as mobile broadband.

1 Decide where and how you want to access the Internet.

2 Decide whether speed matters to you.

3 Decide whether cost plays a large role in your decision.

4 Call the companies that offer the service you want.

DID YOU KNOW?
Each Internet option offers varying rate plans, which may be calculated based on how often you go online, whether or not you have an existing service with the provider, such as a mobile phone, cable TV or digital phone, and how much bandwidth you use, which reflects the amount of data you send and receive.

HOT TIP: If you want to connect only from home, consider a cable, broadband or DSL connection.

ALERT: If you don't have access to broadband, you'll have to go with a wireless or dial-up connection.

DID YOU KNOW?
You can visit a website such as www.broadband-finder.co.uk to compare prices and services.

HOT TIP: If you want to connect from anywhere, consider a mobile phone or wireless satellite provider.

HOT TIP: Consider using your existing mobile phone, cable or satellite TV provider. Many offer bundled pricing.

Check for a wireless network card

If you have a laptop and don't want to pay for Internet service, you can take your laptop to a free Internet hotspot and connect to the Internet at no cost. However, your laptop must have the required wireless hardware. You can find out whether you have this hardware using Device Manager.

1 Click Start.

2 In the Start Search dialogue box, type Device Manager.

3 Under Programs, click Device Manager to open it.

4 Locate Network adapters. (Wireless hardware are called network adapters.)

5 Click the plus sign to expand it – it will become a minus sign as shown here.

6 Locate a device with the word 'wireless' in it.

7 If you see a wireless adapter listed, you have the proper hardware for connecting to a hotspot.

8 Click the X in the top right corner of Device Manager to close it.

> **SEE ALSO:** For more on opening an application, see Chapter 2.

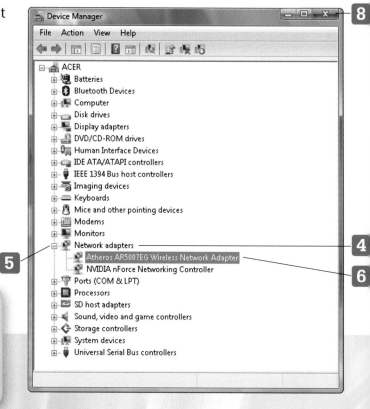

> **? DID YOU KNOW?**
> Even if you have no adapters, you can purchase a USB converter to obtain satellite Internet or a modem to use dial-up.

Obtain the proper settings

Once you've decided on an ISP, you'll need to call the company to set up the subscription. There are some important things to ask the representative, and you must write these things down and keep them in a safe place.

- User name – used to log on to the Internet.
- Email address – used to send and receive email.
- Password – used to secure your Internet connection.
- Incoming POP3 server name – used to set up your email account in Windows Mail.
- Outgoing SMTP server name – used to set up your email account in Windows Mail.
- Account name (may be the same as user name) – used to log on to the Internet and to set up your email account.

 HOT TIP: Ask whether the company will be mailing you a cable modem, wireless card, wireless modem or other device. Also, ask whether there's an extra fee for having someone come to your home to set up your connection.

Create a connection

Before you can connect to the Internet, you need to install any hardware you have received. This may mean connecting a cable modem, wireless access point or DSL modem. Once the hardware is set up, you'll need to access the Network and Sharing Center to create the connection yourself.

1 Open the Network and Sharing Center.

2 Under Tasks, click Set up a connection or network.

3 Click Connect to the Internet – Set up a wireless, broadband, or dial-up connection to the Internet. Click Next.

4 Select either Broadband or Dial-up, based on the ISP's connection option, and click Next.

5 Fill in the required information and click Create.

6 Click Connect.

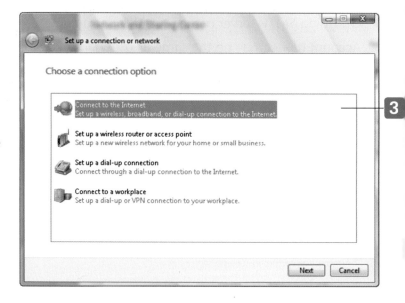

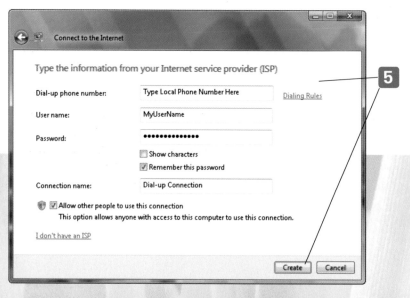

Enable network discovery

Network discovery tells Vista that you're interested in seeing, and possibly joining, other networks. With a laptop, you may want to connect to a public network in your local coffee shop or a private network in your home.

! **ALERT:** You will have to enable Network discovery to be able to view and ultimately join available networks.

1 Open the Network and Sharing Center.

2 Under Sharing and Discovery, click the down arrow next to Off by Network discovery. It will become an up arrow.

3 Click Turn on network discovery, unless it is already turned on.

? **DID YOU KNOW?**
The Network and Sharing Center is also where you set up file sharing, public folder sharing, printer sharing, password protected sharing and media sharing.

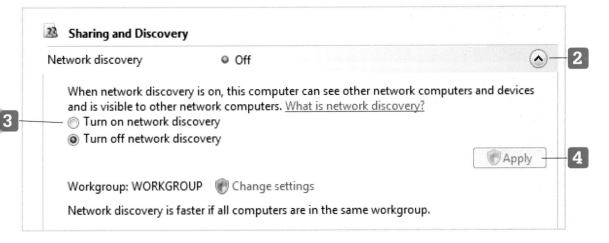

4 Click Apply.

5 Click the X to close the Network and Sharing Center.

? **DID YOU KNOW?**
You can click in the Tasks pane to view computers and devices on your home network and manage network connections.

Diagnose connection problems

If you are having trouble connecting to the Internet through a public or private network, you can diagnose Internet problems using the Network and Sharing Center.

ALERT: If you are connected to the Internet, you will see a green line between your computer and the Internet. If you are not connected, you will see a red X.

1 Open the Network and Sharing Center.

2 To diagnose a non-working Internet connection, click Diagnose and repair.

3 Click the first solution to resolve the connectivity problem.

4 Often, the problem is resolved. If it is not, move to the next step and the next until it is sorted out.

5 Click the X in the top right corner of the Network and Sharing Center window to close it.

DID YOU KNOW?
There are additional troubleshooting tips in the Help and Support pages. Click Start and then Help and Support.

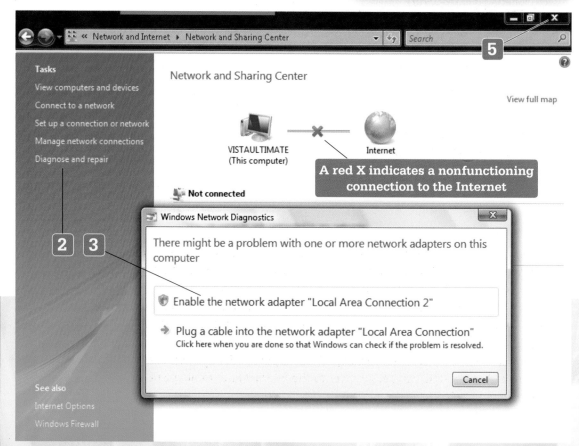

A red X indicates a nonfunctioning connection to the Internet

Join a network

When you connect a new PC running Windows Vista to a wired network or get within range of a wireless one, Vista will find the network and then ask you what kind of network it is. It's a public network if you're in a coffee shop, library or café, and it's a private network if it's a network that you manage, such as a network in your home.

1 Connect physically to a wired network using an Ethernet cable or, if you have wireless hardware installed in your laptop, get within range of a wireless network.

2 Select Home, Work or Public location. (If necessary, input your credentials.)

? DID YOU KNOW?

Connecting to an existing network allows you to access shared features of the network. In a coffee shop that's likely to be only a connection to the Internet; if it's a home network, it's your personal shared data and probably a connection to the Internet too.

🔥 HOT TIP: When a network is accessible, because you've connected to it either using an Ethernet cable or through a wireless network card inside your PC, the Set Network Location wizard will appear.

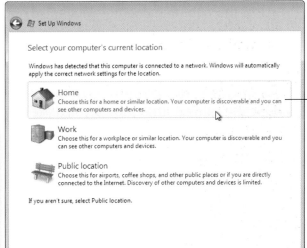

WHAT DOES THIS MEAN?

Home: Choose this if the network is your home network or a network you trust, such as a network at a friend's house. This connection type lets your computer discover other PCs, printers and devices on the network – and they can 'see' you.

Work: Choose this if you are connecting to a network at work. The settings for work and home are the same, but the titles differ so you can tell them apart easily.

Public location: Choose this if the network you want to connect to is open to anyone within range of it, such as a network in a coffee shop, airport or library. Vista assumes that, if you choose Public, you only want to connect to the Internet and nothing else. It closes down discoverability, so that even your shared data are safe.

Open a website in Internet Explorer

Windows Vista comes with Internet Explorer, an application you can use to surf the Internet. Internet Explorer is a Web browser, and it has everything you need, including a pop-up blocker, zoom settings and the ability to save your favourite webpages.

1 Open Internet Explorer. A website will likely open automatically.

2 To open a new website, drag your mouse across the website name to select it. Do not drag your mouse over the http://www part of the address.

3 Type the name of the website you'd like to visit in the address bar. Try amazon.com.

4 Press Enter on the keyboard.

SEE ALSO: Opening an application is covered in Chapter 2.

HOT TIP: You can open Internet Explorer in a number of different ways; just look for the blue E.

ALERT: Websites almost always start with http://www.

? DID YOU KNOW?
.com is the most popular website ending for US companies. The suffix means the website is a company, business or personal website. .edu is used for educational institutions, .gov for government entities, .org mostly for non-profit organisations, and .net for miscellaneous businesses and companies and personal websites. There are other endings too, including .info, .biz, .tv and .uk.com.

WHAT DOES THIS MEAN?
Address bar: Used to type in Internet addresses, also known as URLs (universal resource locators). Generally, an Internet address takes the form of http://www.*companyname*.com.

Open a website in a new tab

You can open more than one website at a time in Internet Explorer. To do this, click the tab that appears to the right of the open webpage. Then, type the name of the website you'd like to visit.

1 Open Internet Explorer.

2 Click an empty tab.

3 Type the name of the website you'd like to visit in the address bar.

4 Press Enter on the keyboard.

HOT TIP: Type the following: http://www.microsoft.com/uk.

? DID YOU KNOW?

When a website name starts with https://, it means it's secure. When purchasing items online, make sure the payment pages have this prefix.

WHAT DOES THIS MEAN?

Command bar: Used to access icons such as the Home and Print icons.

Tabs: Used to access websites when multiple sites are open.

Search window: Used to search for anything on the Internet.

Set a home page

You can select a single webpage or multiple webpages to be displayed each time you open Internet Explorer.

1 Use the address bar to locate a webpage that you want to use as your home page.

2 Click the arrow next to the Home icon.

3 Click Add or Change Home Page.

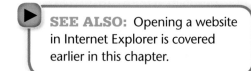

SEE ALSO: Opening a website in Internet Explorer is covered earlier in this chapter.

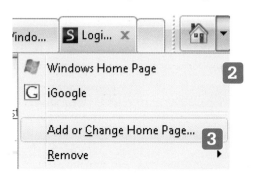

ALERT: You have to locate the webpage before you can assign it as a home page.

4 Make a selection using the information provided regarding each option.

5 Click Yes.

6 Repeat these steps as desired.

WHAT DOES THIS MEAN?

Use this webpage as your only home page: Select this option if you want only one page to serve as your home page.

Add this webpage to your home pages tabs: Select this option if you want this page to be one of several home pages.

Use the current tab set as your home page: Select this option if you've opened multiple tabs and you want all of them to be home pages.

Mark a favourite

Favourites are websites to which you save links so you can access them easily at a later time. Favourites differ from home pages because, by default, they do not open when you start Internet Explorer.

1 Go to the webpage you want to configure as a favourite.

2 Click the Add to Favorites icon.

3 To add a single webpage as a favourite, click Add to Favorites.

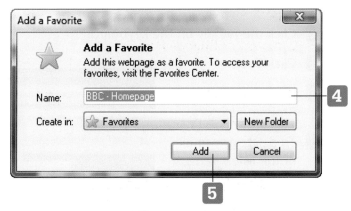

4 Type a name for the website when prompted.

5 Click Add.

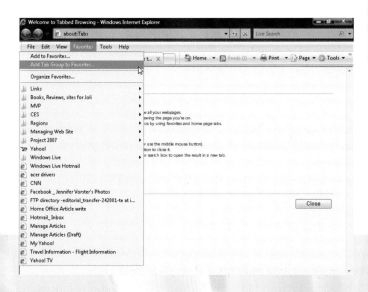

> **HOT TIP:** You can open multiple pages and then add all open websites (every tab that's open) as a tab group. That's what Add Tab Group to Favorites is for.

> **HOT TIP:** You can organise your favourites in your personal Favorites folder.

> **? DID YOU KNOW?**
> The favourites you save appear in the Favorites Center, which you can access by clicking the large yellow star on the Command bar.

Clear history

If you don't want people to be able to snoop around on your computer and find out what sites you've been visiting, you'll need to delete your browsing history. Deleting your browsing history lets you remove the information stored on your computer related to your Internet activities.

1 Open Internet Explorer.

2 Click the Alt key on the keyboard.

3 Click Tools.

4 Click Delete Browsing History.

5 To delete any or all of the listed items, click the Delete button.

6 Click Close when finished.

ALERT: Clicking the Alt key on the keyboard is what causes the menu bar to appear.

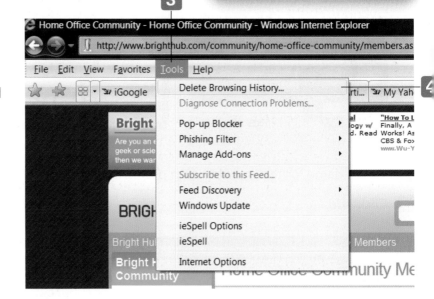

WHAT DOES THIS MEAN?

Temporary Internet Files: These are files that have been downloaded and saved in your Temporary Internet Files folder. A snooper could go through these files to see what you've been doing online.

Cookies: These are small text files that include data to identify your preferences when you visit particular websites. Cookies allow you to visit, say, www.amazon.com and be greeted with *Hello <your name>, We have recommendations for you!* Cookies help a site offer you a personalised Web experience.

History: This is the list of websites you've visited and any Web addresses you've typed. Anyone can look at your history list to see where you've been.

Form data: This is information that's been saved using Internet Explorer's autocomplete form data functionality. If you don't want forms to be filled out automatically by you or someone else who has access to your PC and user account, delete this option.

Passwords: This refers to passwords that were saved using Internet Explorer autocomplete password prompts.

Stay safe online

Chapter 11 in this book is about security. In that chapter, you'll learn how to use Windows Firewall, Windows Defender and other Security Center features. However, much of staying secure when online and surfing the Internet has more to do with common sense.

1 If you are connecting to a public network, make sure you select Public when prompted by Windows Vista.

2 Always keep your PCs secure with antivirus software.

3 Limit the amount of confidential information you store on the Internet.

4 When making credit-card purchases and travel reservations online, always make sure the website address starts with https://.

5 Always sign out of any secure website you enter.

Joli Ballew | **Edit Profile** | Writer Dashboard | Sign out

6 Keep drinks, pets and cigarette smoke away from your PC.

? DID YOU KNOW?
When you connect to a network you know, such as a network in your home, you should select Home or Work.

! ALERT: You have to purchase and install your own antivirus software, as it does not come with Vista.

! ALERT: Don't put your address and phone number on Facebook and other social networking sites.

 HOT TIP: The 's' after 'http' lets you know it's a *secure* site.

WHAT DOES THIS MEAN?

Link: A shortcut to a webpage. Links are often offered in emails, documents and webpages to allow you to access sites without having to actually type in their names. In almost all instances, links are underlined and in a different colour than the page they are configured on.

Load: A web page must load before you can access it. Some pages load instantly, while others take a few seconds.

Navigate: The process of moving from one webpage to another or viewing items on a single webpage. Often the term is used as follows: 'Click the link to navigate to the new webpage.'

Search: A term used when you type a word or group of words into a search window. Searching for data produces results.

Scroll Up and Scroll Down: A process of using the scroll bars on a webpage or the arrow keys on a keyboard to move up and down the pages of a website.

Website: A group of webpages that contains related information. Microsoft's website contains information about Microsoft products, for instance.

URL: The text you type to access a website, such as http://www.microsoft.com.

8 Working with email

Introduction

Windows Mail is installed on your laptop. It's included in all editions of Microsoft Windows Vista, and it is the only thing you need to view, send and receive email, manage your contacts, and manage sent, saved and incoming email. Within Windows Mail you can print email, create folders for storing email that you want to keep, manage unwanted email, open attachments, send pictures inside email and more.

To use Windows Mail, you need an email address and two email server addresses, all of which you can get from your ISP. In fact, you probably have this information already if you worked through Chapter 7. With this information to hand, you'll work through the New Connection Wizard, inputting the required information when prompted, to set up the program. Once Mail is set up, you're ready to send and receive mail. Don't worry, it's easy!

Set up an email account in Mail

The first time you open Windows Mail, you'll be prompted to input the required information regarding your email address and email servers. That's because Windows Mail is a program for sending and receiving email, and you can't do that without inputting the proper information.

1   Click Start, and click Windows Mail.

2   Click E-mail Account. Click Next.

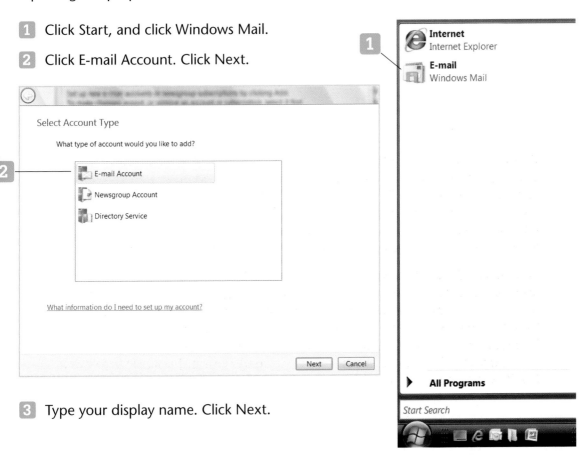

3   Type your display name. Click Next.

WHAT DOES THIS MEAN?

Display name: This is the name that will appear in the From field when you compose an email, and in the recipient's inbox (under 'From' in their email list) when they receive email from you. Don't put your email address here; put your first and last name, and any additional information.

Email address: This is the email address you chose when you signed up with your ISP. It often takes this form: *yourname@yourispname.com*.

E-Mail user name and password: Often your user name is your email address. Passwords are a security measure and are case-sensitive.

4 Type your email address. Click Next.

5 Fill in the information for your incoming and outgoing mail servers. Click Next.

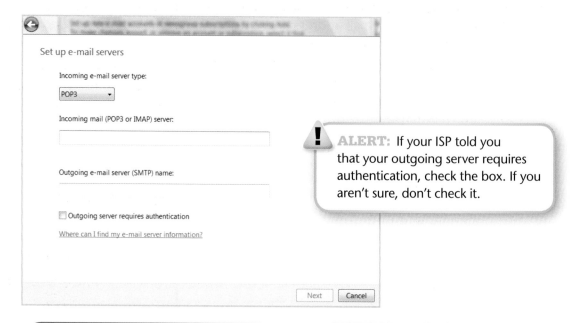

ALERT: If your ISP told you that your outgoing server requires authentication, check the box. If you aren't sure, don't check it.

WHAT DOES THIS MEAN?
Mail server: The name of the computer that handles your incoming and outgoing email.

ALERT: If you don't know what to type, call your ISP or visit their website.

6 Type your email user name and password. Click Next.

HOT TIP: Leave Remember Password checked so that Mail remembers it.

ALERT: To resolve errors, in the Internet Accounts dialogue box, which will still be available, click the email address to repair and then click Properties.

7 Click Finish.

View an email

Windows Mail checks for email automatically when you first open the program and every 30 minutes thereafter. If you want to check for email manually, you can click the Send/Receive button any time you want. When you receive mail, there are two ways to read it. You can click the message once and read it in the Mail window, or you can double-click it to open it in its own window.

 HOT TIP: I think it's best to simply click the email once. That way you don't have multiple open windows to deal with.

1 Click the Send/Receive button.

2 Click the email once.

3 View the contents of the email.

ALERT: Email is received in the Inbox. If Inbox is not selected, you must select it first!

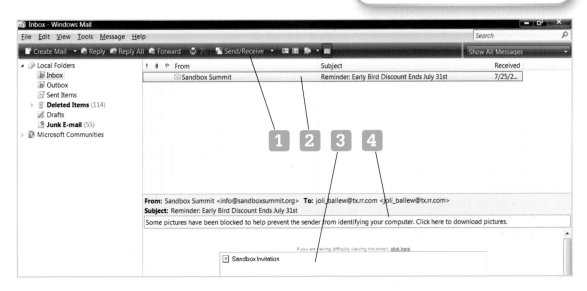

4 If there are pictures in the email but you can't see them, click the yellow bar.

WHAT DOES THIS MEAN?
Spam: Junk email, unwanted email and sales ads.

ALERT: Click to view pictures only if you know the sender. If you view the pictures in a spam message, the spammer will know that your email address works and then send you more spam.

 HOT TIP: You can also adjust the size of the panes by dragging the grey border between any of them up or down.

Change how often Mail checks for email

You may want to have Mail check for email more or less often than every 30 minutes. It's easy to make the change.

1 Click Tools.

2 Click Options.

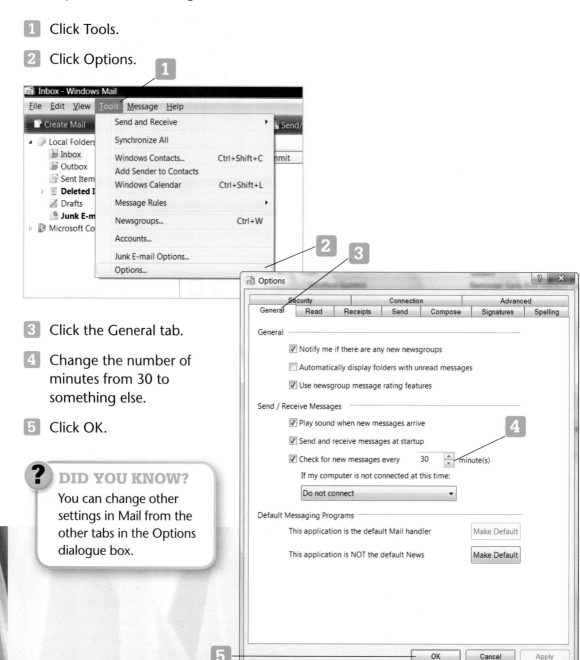

3 Click the General tab.

4 Change the number of minutes from 30 to something else.

5 Click OK.

? DID YOU KNOW?

You can change other settings in Mail from the other tabs in the Options dialogue box.

View an attachment

An attachment is a file that you can send within an email, such as a picture, document or video clip. If an email message you receive contains an attachment, you'll see a paperclip. To open the attachment, click the paperclip icon in the Preview pane, and click the attachment's name.

1 Click the email once in the Message pane.

2 Click the paperclip in the Preview pane.

3 Click the name of the attachment.

4 Click Open.

ALERT: Hackers send attachments that look like they are from legitimate companies, such as banks and online services. Be very careful when opening these and make sure you know the email is from a legitimate source.

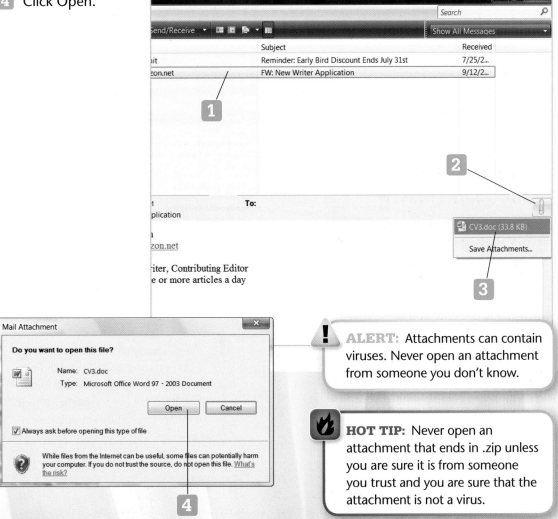

ALERT: Attachments can contain viruses. Never open an attachment from someone you don't know.

HOT TIP: Never open an attachment that ends in .zip unless you are sure it is from someone you trust and you are sure that the attachment is not a virus.

Recover email from the Junk E-mail folder

Windows Mail has a junk email filter, and anything it thinks is spam gets sent there. Unfortunately, sometimes email gets sent to the Junk E-mail folder that is actually legitimate email. Therefore, once a week or so, you should look in this folder to see whether any email you want to keep is in there.

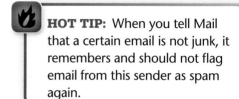

HOT TIP: When you tell Mail that a certain email is not junk, it remembers and should not flag email from this sender as spam again.

1 Click the Junk E-mail folder once.

2 Use the scroll bars if necessary to browse through the email messages in the folder.

3 If you see an email that is legitimate, click it once.

4 Click Not Junk.

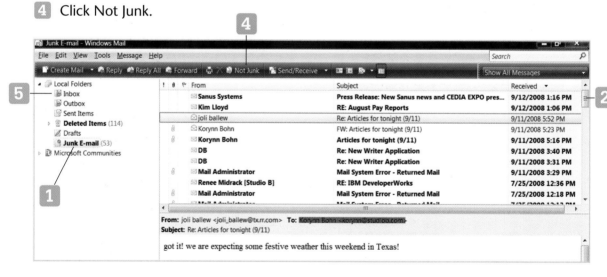

5 After reviewing the files, click Inbox.

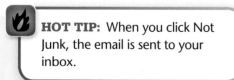

HOT TIP: When you click Not Junk, the email is sent to your inbox.

ALERT: Mail requires routine maintenance, including deleting email from the Junk E-mail folder. You'll learn how to delete items in a folder later in this chapter.

Reply to an email

When someone sends you an email, you may need to send a reply back to them. You do that by selecting the email and then clicking the Reply button.

1 Select the email you want to reply to in the Message pane.

2 Click Reply.

> **! ALERT:** If the email you are replying to was sent to you along with additional people, clicking Reply will send a reply to the person who composed the message. Clicking Reply All will send the reply to everyone who received the email.

3 In the To field, type the email address for the recipient.

4 Type a subject in the Subject field.

5 Type the message in the body pane.

6 Click Send.

> **🔥 HOT TIP:** To send a single email to multiple recipients, separate each email address with a semicolon.

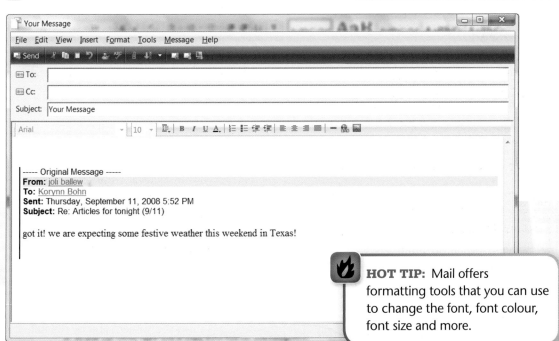

> **🔥 HOT TIP:** Mail offers formatting tools that you can use to change the font, font colour, font size and more.

Forward an email

When someone sends you an email that you want to share with others, you can forward the email. You do this by selecting the email and then clicking the Forward button.

1 Select the email you want to forward in the Message pane.

2 Click Forward.

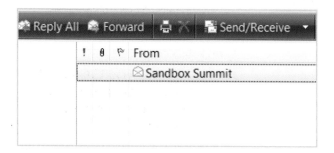

3 In the To field, type the email address for the recipient.

4 Type a subject in the Subject field.

5 Type the message in the body pane.

6 Click Send.

> **? DID YOU KNOW?**
> People often forward funny jokes.

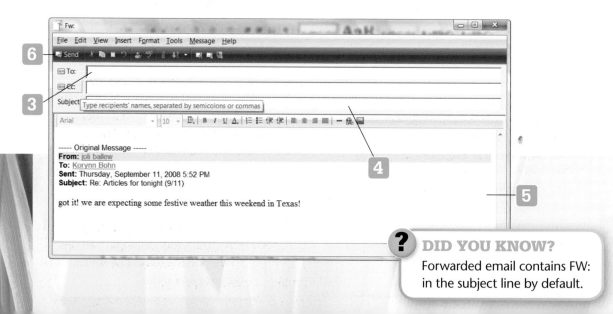

> **? DID YOU KNOW?**
> Forwarded email contains FW: in the subject line by default.

Compose and send a new email

You compose an email message by clicking Create Mail on the toolbar. You input who the email should be sent to, type the subject, and then you write the message.

1 Click Create Mail.

2 Type the recipient's email address in the To line. If you want to add additional names, separate each email address with a semicolon.

3 Type a subject in the Subject field.

4 Type the message in the body pane.

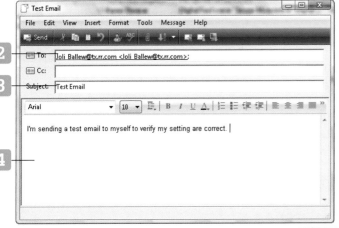

5 Click Send.

? DID YOU KNOW?

In Mail there's a menu bar and a toolbar, which you can use to access other features, including tools you may already be familiar with, such as cut, copy, paste, spell check, font, font size, font colour and font style.

HOT TIP: Select Tools, and click Select Recipients to add email addresses from your address book.

HOT TIP: Make sure the subject adequately describes the body of your email. Your recipients should be able to review the subject line later and be able to recall what the email was about.

? DID YOU KNOW?

If you want to send the email to someone and you don't need them to respond, you can put them in the Cc line.

? DID YOU KNOW?

If you want to send the email to someone and you don't want other recipients to know you included them in the email, add them to the Bcc line. (You can show this line by clicking View and then clicking All Headers.)

WHAT DOES THIS MEAN?

Cc: Stands for carbon copy.
Bcc: Stands for blind carbon copy and is a secret copy.

? DID YOU KNOW?

You can choose Tools and then click Select Recipients to choose multiple recipients from your Contacts list. This way you can add multiple recipients quickly.

Attach a picture to an email using Insert

Although email that contains only text serves its purpose quite a bit of the time, often you'll want to send a photograph, a short video, a sound recording, a document or other data. When you want to include something in your message other than text, you add an attachment. There are many ways to attach something to an email. One way is to use the Insert menu and then choose File Attachment. Then you can browse to the location of the attachment and click Insert.

HOT TIP: When inserting (adding) files to an email, hold down the Ctrl key to select non-contiguous files, and hold down the Shift key to select contiguous files.

1 Click Create Mail.

2 Click Insert.

3 Click File Attachment.

4 If the item you want to attach is saved in your Documents folder, skip to step 6.

5 If the item you want to attach is not in the Documents folder, browse to the location of the folder.

6 Click the item that you want to add, and select Open.

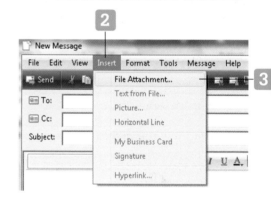

DID YOU KNOW?

If you can locate the file that you want to attach, you can drag the file to the email in progress.

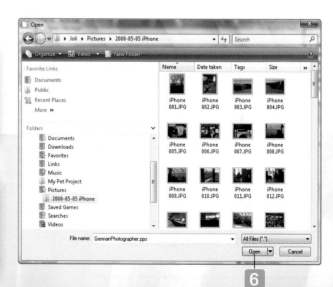

ALERT: Anything that you attach won't be removed from your computer; instead, a copy will be created for the attachment.

Attach a picture to an email using right-click

You can create an email that contains an attachment by right-clicking the file you want to attach. This method attaches the files to a new email, which is fine if you want to create a new email. The only problem with this is that it doesn't work when you send forwards and replies. However, this method has a feature other methods don't: with this method, you can resize any images you've selected before you send them. This is a great perk because many pictures are too large to send via email; resizing them helps you manage an email's size.

1 Locate the file you'd like to attach and right-click it.

2 Point to Send To.

3 Click Mail Recipient.

4 If the item you're attaching is a picture, choose the picture size.

5 Click Attach.

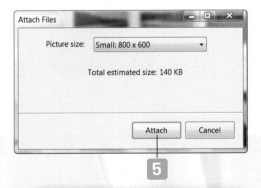

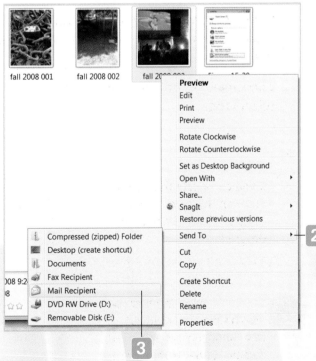

Add a contact

A contact is a data file that holds the information you keep about a person. The contact information looks like a contact card. The information may include a picture, email address, postal address, first and last names and similar data. You can import contacts when prompted during Mail's set up process, manually add a contact to the address by typing the required information into the Address Book, add contacts by synching mobile devices like mobile phones or a number of other ways.

1 From Windows Mail, click the Contacts icon on the toolbar.

Contacts

2 Click New Contact.

3 Type all of the information you want to add. Be sure to add information to each tab.

4 Click OK.

Print an email

Sometimes you'll need to print an email or its attachment. Windows Mail makes it easy to print. Just click the printer icon on the toolbar. After clicking the Print icon, the Print dialogue box will appear, where you can select a printer, set print preferences, choose a page range and print.

1 Select the email to print by clicking the email in the Message pane.

2 Click the Print icon.

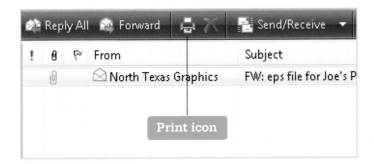

3 In the Print dialogue box, select the printer to use, if more than one exists.

4 Click Print.

You can configure print preferences and choose what pages to print using Preferences. Refer to your printer's user manual to find out what print options your printer supports.

 HOT TIP: You should see a printer icon appear on the right side of the taskbar during the print task. Click the icon for more information.

Apply a junk mail filter

Just as you receive unwanted information from telephone marketers, radio stations and television ads, you're going to get unwanted advertisements in emails. This is referred to as junk email or spam. Most of these advertisements are scams and rip-offs; some contain pornographic images. There are four filtering options in Windows Mail: No Automatic Filtering, Low, High, and Safe List Only.

1 Click Tools.

2 Click Junk E-mail Options.

3 From the Options tab, make a selection. We suggest starting at Low and moving to High if necessary later.

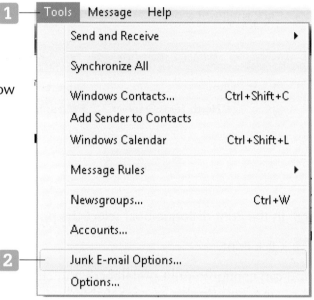

WHAT DOES THIS MEAN?

No Automatic Filtering: Use this option only if you do not want Windows Mail to block junk email messages. Windows Mail will continue to block messages from email addresses listed on the Blocked Senders list.

Low: Use this option if you receive very little junk email. You can start here and increase the filter if it becomes necessary.

High: Use this option if you receive a lot of junk email and want to block as much of it as possible. Use this option for children's email accounts. Note that some valid email will likely be blocked, so you'll have to review the junk email folder occasionally to make sure you aren't missing any email you actually want to keep.

Safe List Only: Use this option if you only want to receive messages from people or domain names on your Safe Senders list. This is a drastic step and requires you to add every sender from whom you want to receive mail to the Safe Senders list. Use this as a last resort.

4 Click the Phishing tab.

5 Select Protect my Inbox from messages with potential Phishing links. Additionally, move phishing email to the Junk E-mail folder.

6 Click OK.

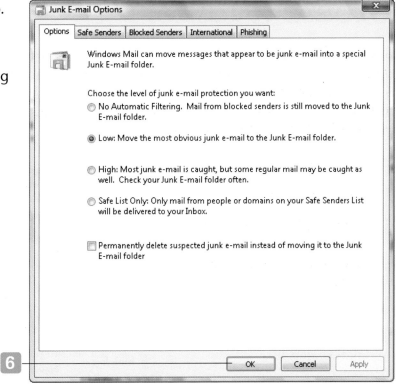

 ALERT: Never buy anything from a junk email, send money to a sick or dying person who you don't know, send money for your portion of a lottery ticket, or fall for other spam hoaxes.

ALERT: Don't give your email address to any website or company, or include it in any registration card, unless you're willing to receive junk email from them and their constituents.

ALERT: Check the junk email folder often to make sure no legitimate email has been moved there.

SEE ALSO: Recovering email from the Junk E-mail folder is covered earlier in this chapter.

Create a folder

It's important to perform some housekeeping chores once a month or so. If you don't, Windows Mail may get bogged down and perform more slowly than it should, or you may be unable to manage the email you want to keep. One way to keep Mail under control is to create a new folder to hold email that you want to keep and then move mail into it.

1 Right-click Local Folders.

2 Select New Folder.

3 Type a name for the new folder.

4 Select Local Folders.

5 Click OK.

6 Note the new folder in the Local Folders list.

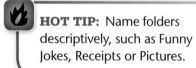

HOT TIP: Name folders descriptively, such as Funny Jokes, Receipts or Pictures.

? DID YOU KNOW?
Using the same technique, you can create subfolders inside folders.

Move email to a folder

Moving an email from one folder, such as your inbox, to another, such as Funny Jokes, is a simple task. Just drag the email from one folder to the other.

1 Right-click the email message that you want to move in the Message pane.

2 Hold down the mouse button while dragging the message to the new folder.

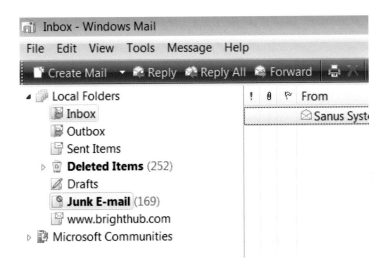

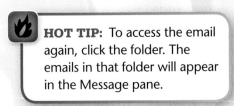

HOT TIP: To access the email again, click the folder. The emails in that folder will appear in the Message pane.

Delete email in a folder

In order to keep Mail from getting full, you'll need to delete email in folders occasionally. Depending on how much email you get, this may be as often as once a week.

1 Right-click Junk E-mail.

2 Click Empty 'Junk E-mail' Folder.

3 Right-click Deleted Items.

4 Click Empty 'Deleted Items' Folder.

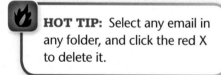 **HOT TIP:** Select any email in any folder, and click the red X to delete it.

9 Share data and printers

Introduction

If you have a PC in addition to your laptop, you will probably want to share data between them. If your home PC has a printer, you may want to print with the same printer from your laptop when connected to your local network. Vista lets you share resources and data on your network. However, you must turn on sharing features, because by default, sharing is not enabled. Once you've turned on sharing, you can share a personal folder, view and manage your shared data, and access shared printers.

Open the Network and Sharing Center

The Network and Sharing Center is where you tell Vista what you want to share with others on your network and others who have access to your laptop.

1 Click Start.

2 In the Start Search window, type Network and Sharing.

> **?** **DID YOU KNOW?**
> You can also simply type Network in the Start Search window.

3 Under Programs, click Network and Sharing Center.

4 The Network and Sharing Center opens.

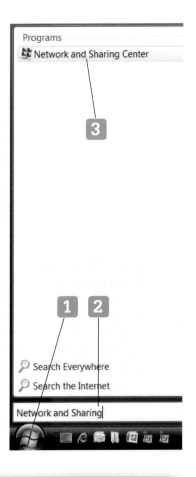

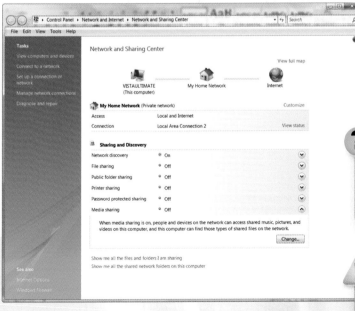

> **?** **DID YOU KNOW?**
> Network discovery must be turned on in order for your PC to find other PCs and to share data.

> **!** **ALERT:** Notice the down arrows in the list. Clicking them offers more information about each section.

Turn on file sharing

When you turn on file sharing, data that you have shared are accessible by others on your local network.

1 Open the Network and Sharing Center.

2 Click the down arrow by File sharing.

3 Click Turn on file sharing.

4 Click Apply.

ALERT: Network discovery must be enabled for you to join a network.

SEE ALSO: Enable network discovery is covered in Chapter 7.

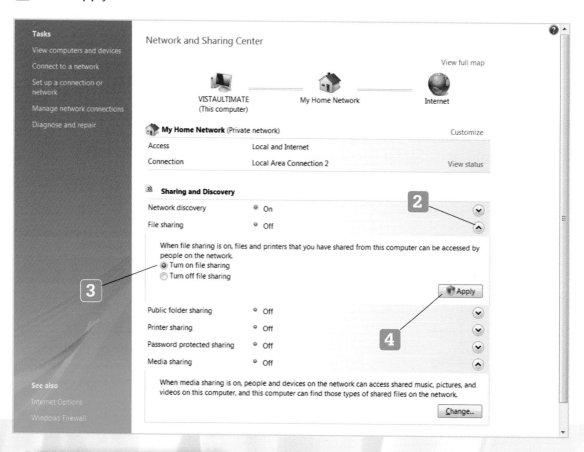

DID YOU KNOW?

When you turn on file sharing, Public folder sharing is also enabled in read-only mode.

WHAT DOES THIS MEAN?

Read only: A security feature applied to folders. Users with access to the folder can read the contents, but they cannot make changes to or delete the data.

Turn on printer sharing

When you turn on printer sharing, printers that you have shared are accessible by others on your local network. You must turn on printer sharing in order for other PCs to obtain access to your shared printers.

1. Open the Network and Sharing Center.

2. Click the down arrow by Printer sharing.

3. Click Turn on printer sharing.

4. Click Apply.

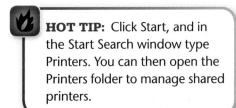

HOT TIP: Click Start, and in the Start Search window type Printers. You can then open the Printers folder to manage shared printers.

Printer sharing   ○ Off

When printer sharing is on, people with network access can connect to and use printers attached to this computer.
- ◉ Turn on printer sharing
- ○ Turn off printer sharing

Apply

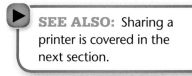

SEE ALSO: Sharing a printer is covered in the next section.

Share a printer

After turning on printer sharing, you'll need to manually share the printer(s) that you want others to have access to. This printer is probably installed on your desktop PC.

ALERT: These instructions are Vista-specific. If your desktop PC runs XP, the steps are slightly different.

1. Click Start, and in the Start Search window type Printers.

2. Under Programs, click Printers.

3. Locate the printer to share.

ALERT: Your PC and printer will need to be turned on in order for others to access the shared printer.

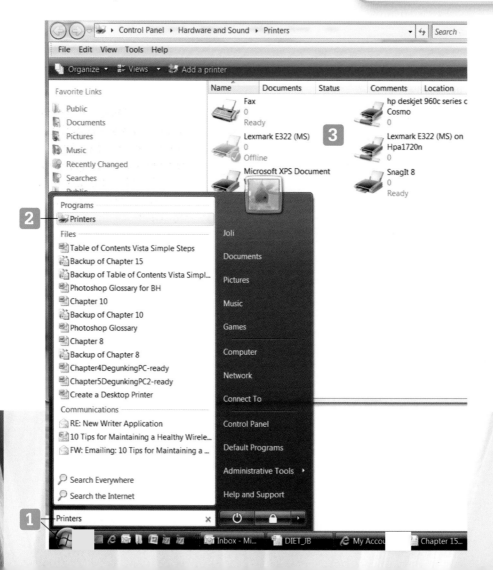

4 Right-click the printer, and click Sharing.

5 Click Share this printer.

6 Click OK.

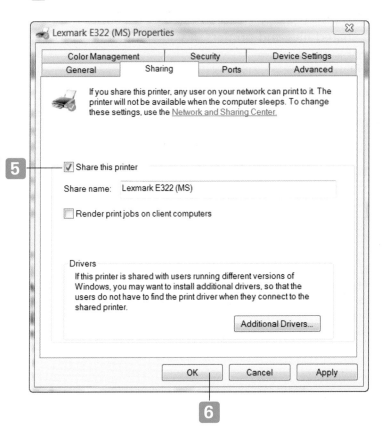

5

6

> ⚠ **ALERT:** When others on your network access the printer for the first time, they may be prompted to install a driver for it. This is OK and will be managed by the PC.

Turn on password-protected sharing

When password-protected sharing is on, only people who have a user account and a password on your laptop can access shared files and printers. If you want all users to input a user name and password, enable this feature.

1 Open the Network and Sharing Center.

2 Click the down arrow by Password protected sharing.

3 Click Turn on password protected sharing and click Apply.

! ALERT: Users who have a user name but not a password will not be able to access files until they apply a password to their account.

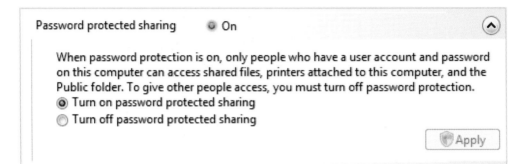

Password protected sharing   ◉ On   ⌃

When password protection is on, only people who have a user account and password on this computer can access shared files, printers attached to this computer, and the Public folder. To give other people access, you must turn off password protection.
◉ Turn on password protected sharing
◯ Turn off password protected sharing

Apply

! ALERT: This feature does not have to be turned on in order to share files and folders.

Share a personal folder

Sometimes you won't want to move or copy data into Public folders and subfolders. Instead, you'll want to share data directly from your own personal folders. To do this, you'll have to share the desired personal folders.

 HOT TIP: You may want to share your own Pictures folder instead of copying or moving the files into the Public Pictures folder.

1 Locate the folder to share.

2 Right-click the folder.

3 Choose Share.

4 Click the down arrow shown here, and select any user (or Everyone) to share the folder with.

5 Click Add.

6 Click the arrow next to the new user name.

7 Select a sharing option.

8 Click Share.

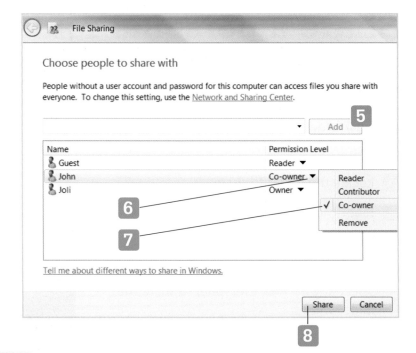

 HOT TIP: To view all of your shared files, open the Network and Sharing Center and click View all of the files and folders I am sharing.

WHAT DOES THIS MEAN?

Owner: This is the person who created the file, uploaded the picture, purchased or ripped the music, or saved the video.

Co-owner: This is a person who has owner permissions, and can thus edit, delete and add files to the folder.

Reader: This is a person who can only access what's in the folder and cannot edit it.

10 Change system defaults

Introduction

Vista comes preconfigured with certain settings, called system defaults. These include things such as how folders look on the screen, and the date and time. You can make changes to these defaults and other settings and what shows on the taskbar.

Change AutoPlay settings

Your laptop doesn't know what you want it to do when you insert a blank CD, a DVD movie or a music CD, so most of the time it asks you by offering up a dialogue box. You can tell Vista what you want it to do when you insert or access media though, thus bypassing the prompt and getting right to the music, picture or DVD that you want to view.

1 Click Start.

2 Click Default Programs. (It's on the Start menu.)

3 Click Change AutoPlay settings.

HOT TIP: You can change AutoPlay settings to configure what program should be used to open what type of media.

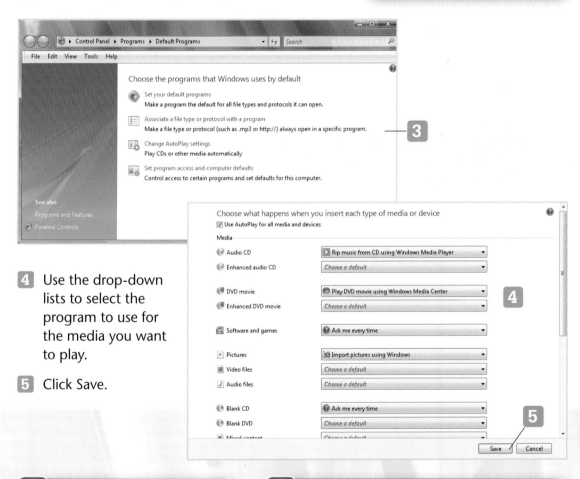

4 Use the drop-down lists to select the program to use for the media you want to play.

5 Click Save.

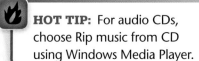

HOT TIP: For audio CDs, choose Rip music from CD using Windows Media Player.

HOT TIP: For DVD movies, choose Play DVD movie using Windows Media Center (if you're running Home Premium or Ultimate).

Change the date and time

Laptops are great for travelling, and immersing yourself in the local culture adds to the experience. When travelling, you'll probably want to change the date and time, or at least the time zone, and you can do so from the Date and Time dialogue box.

1 Click Start.

2 Click Control Panel.

3 Click Clock, Language and Region.

4 Click Set the time and date.

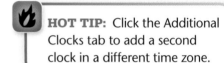

HOT TIP: Click the Additional Clocks tab to add a second clock in a different time zone.

Date and Time
Set the time and date | Change the time zone | Add clocks for different time zones
Add the Clock gadget to Windows Sidebar

5 Click Change date and time.

6 Use the arrows or type in a new time.

7 Select a new date.

8 Click OK.

9 Click OK.

HOT TIP: Choose Change the time zone to change the time zone instead of the time.

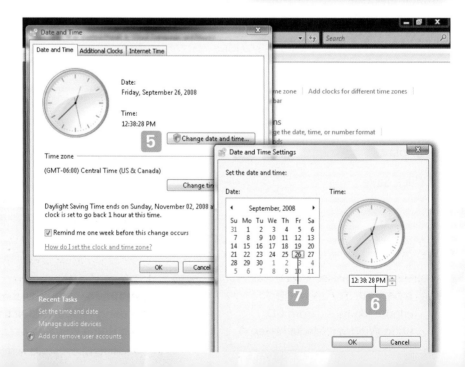

Change language settings

When you travel with a laptop, you may need to change the country or region, and the date, time and number format. If you speak and work in multiple languages, you may also need to change keyboards or other input methods. You can do this from the Control Panel.

1 Click Start.

2 Click Control Panel.

3 Click Clock, Language and Region.

4 Click Regional and Language Options.

5 Make changes as desired from the available drop-down lists.

6 Click OK.

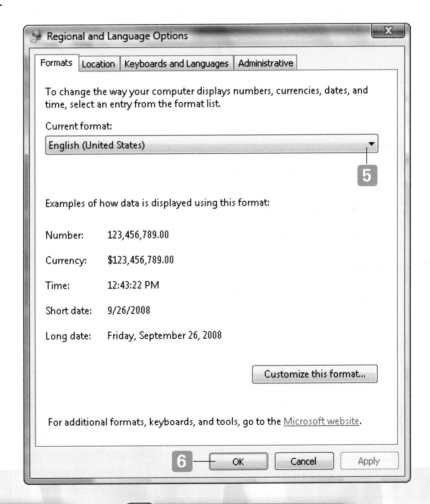

Regional and Language Options

| Formats | Location | Keyboards and Languages | Administrative |

To change the way your computer displays numbers, currencies, dates, and time, select an entry from the format list.

Current format:

English (United States)

5

Examples of how data is displayed using this format:

Number: 123,456,789.00

Currency: $123,456,789.00

Time: 12:43:22 PM

Short date: 9/26/2008

Long date: Friday, September 26, 2008

Customize this format...

For additional formats, keyboards, and tools, go to the Microsoft website.

6 — OK   Cancel   Apply

? DID YOU KNOW?
You can customise any format by clicking the Customize this format button.

🔥 HOT TIP: To set your current location, click the Current Location tab and select the desired country from the drop-down list.

Change folder options

You can change how folders react by configuring Folder Options. You can single-click (instead of double-click) to open a folder, choose to open each folder in its own window, view hidden files and folders, and more.

1 Click Start.

2 In the Start Search window, type Folder Options.

3 Under Programs in the results list, click Folder Options.

4 From the General tab, read the options and make changes as desired.

HOT TIP: If you're more comfortable with older operating systems, choose Use Windows classic folders.

5 From the View tab, read the options and make changes as desired.

6 From the Search tab, read the options and make changes as desired.

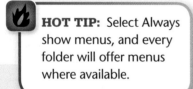

HOT TIP: Select Always show menus, and every folder will offer menus where available.

HOT TIP: To shorten the list of search results, deselect Find partial matches.

Change touchpad and mouse settings

You can change the speed the cursor moves on the screen when you use the touchpad or an external mouse, the shape of the mouse pointer and other settings from their defaults. For example, you can change a right-handed touchpad into a left-handed touchpad using Mouse settings.

1 Click Start, and in the Start Search window type mouse.

2 In the results, under Programs click Mouse.

3 From the Buttons tab, read the options and make changes as desired.

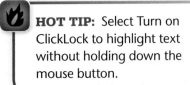

HOT TIP: Select Turn on ClickLock to highlight text without holding down the mouse button.

4 From the Pointers tab, select a theme as desired.

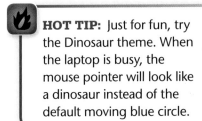

HOT TIP: Just for fun, try the Dinosaur theme. When the laptop is busy, the mouse pointer will look like a dinosaur instead of the default moving blue circle.

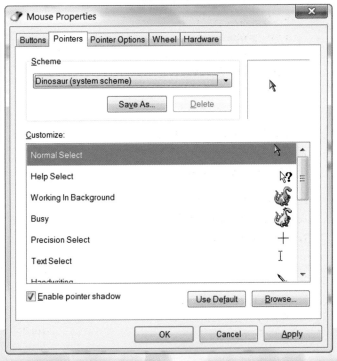

5 From the Pointer Options tab, read the options and make changes as desired.

6 From the Wheel tab, read the options and make changes as desired.

7 Click OK.

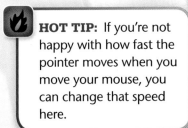

HOT TIP: If you're not happy with how fast the pointer moves when you move your mouse, you can change that speed here.

HOT TIP: Enable Snap To and the cursor will move to the default option in dialogue boxes.

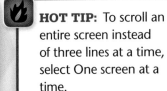

HOT TIP: To scroll an entire screen instead of three lines at a time, select One screen at a time.

11 Stay secure

Introduction

Your laptop comes with a lot of built-in features to keep you and your data safe. Vista security tools and features help you avoid email scams, harmful websites and hackers, and also help you protect your data and your laptop from unscrupulous visitors and nosy family members. If you know how to take advantage of the available safeguards, you'll be protected in almost all cases. You just need to be aware of the dangers, heed security warnings when they are given – and resolve them – and use all of the available features in Vista to protect yourself and your computer.

Add a new user account

You created your user account when you first turned on your new Vista laptop. Your user account is what defines your personal folders as well as your settings for your desktop background, screen saver and other items. You are the administrator of your laptop. If you share the PC with someone, they should have their own user account too.

1 Click Start.

2 Click Control Panel.

3 Click Add or remove user accounts.

4 Click Create a new account.

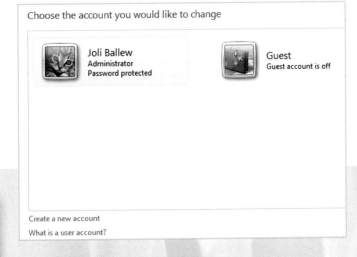

> ⚠ **ALERT:** All accounts should have a password applied to them. Refer to the next section, Require a password, for more on this.

5 Type a new account name.

6 Verify that Standard user is selected.

7 Click Create Account.

? DID YOU KNOW?
Administrators can make changes to system-wide settings, but standard users cannot do so without an administrator's name and password.

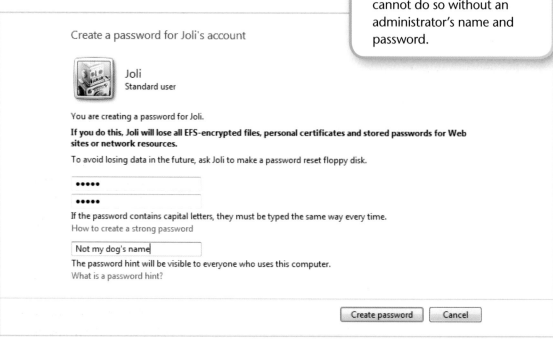

Create a password for Joli's account

Joli
Standard user

You are creating a password for Joli.

If you do this, Joli will lose all EFS-encrypted files, personal certificates and stored passwords for Web sites or network resources.

To avoid losing data in the future, ask Joli to make a password reset floppy disk.

•••••

•••••

If the password contains capital letters, they must be typed the same way every time.
How to create a strong password

Not my dog's name

The password hint will be visible to everyone who uses this computer.
What is a password hint?

[Create password] [Cancel]

8 Click the X in the top right corner to close the window.

! ALERT: If every person who accesses your laptop has their own standard user account and password, and if every person logs on using that account and then logs off the laptop each time they've finished using it, then you'll never have to worry about anyone accessing anyone else's personal data.

HOT TIP: You can also click Change the picture, Change the account name, Remove the password, and other options to further personalise the account.

Require a password

All user accounts, even your own, should be password-protected. When a password is configured, you must type the password to log on to your laptop. This protects the computer from unauthorised access.

1 Click Start.

2 Click Control Panel.

3 Click Add or remove user accounts.

4 Click the user account to which you want to apply a password.

5 Click Create a password.

6 Type the new password, type it again to confirm it, and type a password hint.

7 Click Create password.

8 Click the X in the top right of the window to close it.

? DID YOU KNOW?

When you need to make a system-wide change, you have to be logged on as an administrator or type an administrator's user name and password.

! ALERT: Create a password that contains upper- and lower-case letters and a few numbers. Write the password down and keep it somewhere safe and out of sight.

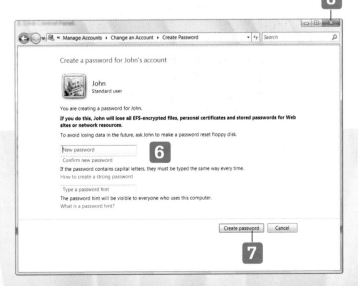

Configure Windows Update

It's very important to configure Windows Update to get and install updates automatically. This is the easiest way to ensure that your laptop is as up-to-date as possible, at least for patching security flaws that Microsoft uncovers, having access to the latest features, and obtaining updates to the operating system itself. I propose you verify that the recommended settings are enabled as detailed here, and then check occasionally for optional updates manually.

1 Click Start.

2 Click Control Panel.

3 Click Security.

4 Click Windows Update.

> ## WHAT DOES THIS MEAN?
> **Windows Update:** If enabled and configured properly, when you are online Vista will check for security updates and install them automatically. You don't have to do anything, and your PC is always updated with the latest security patches and features.

Security
Check for updates
Check this computer's security status
Allow a program through Windows Firewall

> **ALERT:** You may see that optional components or updates are available. You can view these updates and install them if desired.

Windows Update
Turn automatic updating on or off | Check for updates | View installed updates

5 In the left pane, click Change settings.

6 Configure the settings as shown here, and click OK.

> **? DID YOU KNOW?**
> If the laptop is not online at 3 a.m., it will check for updates the next time it is online.

Scan for viruses with Windows Defender

You don't have to do much to Windows Defender, except understand that it offers protection against Internet threats. It's enabled by default and it runs in the background. However, if you ever think that your laptop has been attacked by an Internet threat (virus, worm, malware, etc.), you can run a manual scan here.

1 Click Start.

2 Click Control Panel.

3 Click Security.

4 Click Windows Defender.

Windows Defender
Scan for spyware and other potentially unwanted software

5 Click the arrow next to Scan (not the Scan icon). Click Full Scan if you think the laptop has been infected.

6 Click the X in the top right corner to close the Windows Defender window.

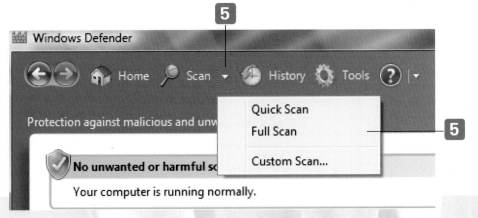

> **WHAT DOES THIS MEAN?**
> **Malware:** Malicious software, such as viruses, worms and spyware.

Enable the firewall

Windows Firewall is a software program that checks the data that comes in from the Internet or a local network and then decides whether the data are good or bad. If the program deems the data harmless, it will allow the data to come through the firewall; if not, it blocks the data.

ALERT: You have to have a firewall to stop hackers from gaining access to your laptop, and to help prevent your laptop from sending out malicious code if it is ever attacked by a virus or worm.

1 Click Start.

2 Click Control Panel.

3 Click Security.

4 Under Windows Firewall, click Turn Windows Firewall on or off.

Windows Firewall
🛡 Turn Windows Firewall on or off   🛡 Allow a program through Windows Firewall

5 Verify that the firewall is On. If not, select On.

6 Click OK.

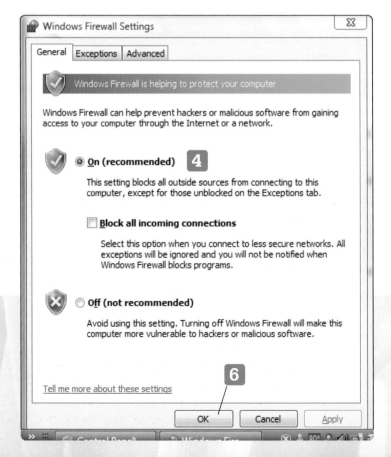

Windows Firewall Settings

General | Exceptions | Advanced

Windows Firewall is helping to protect your computer

Windows Firewall can help prevent hackers or malicious software from gaining access to your computer through the Internet or a network.

◉ **On (recommended)** **4**

This setting blocks all outside sources from connecting to this computer, except for those unblocked on the Exceptions tab.

☐ **Block all incoming connections**

Select this option when you connect to less secure networks. All exceptions will be ignored and you will not be notified when Windows Firewall blocks programs.

○ **Off (not recommended)**

Avoid using this setting. Turning off Windows Firewall will make this computer more vulnerable to hackers or malicious software.

6

Tell me more about these settings

OK | Cancel | Apply

View and resolve Security Center warnings

The Security Center is a talkative application. You'll see a pop-up if your antivirus software is out-of-date or not installed, if you don't have the proper security settings configured, or if Windows Update or the firewall is disabled. You'll also get a user account control prompt each time you want to install a program or make a system-wide change.

1 Click Start.

2 Click Control Panel.

3 Click Security.

4 If there's anything in red or yellow, click the down arrow to see the problem.

5 Note the resolution and perform the task.

ALERT: When you see alerts such as these, pay attention! You need to resolve them.

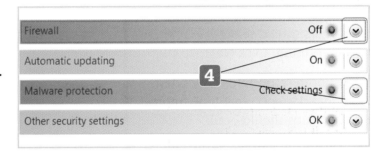

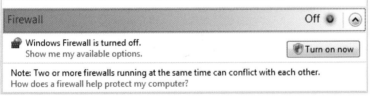

6 Continue in this manner to resolve all Security Center issues.

7 Click the X in the top right corner of the Security Center window to close it.

DID YOU KNOW?
Vista comes with malware protection but not antivirus protection.

ALERT: Install antivirus software to protect your PC from viruses and worms.

WHAT DOES THIS MEAN?

Virus: A self-replicating program that infects computers, including laptops, with intent to do harm. Viruses often come in the form of attachments in emails.

Worm: A self-replicating program that infects computers, including laptops, with intent to do harm. However, unlike a virus, it does not need to attach itself to a running program.

Create a basic back-up

Windows Vista comes with a back-up program that you can use to back up your personal data. The back-up program is located in the Backup and Restore Center.

1 Click Start.

2 Click Control Panel.

3 Click Back up your computer.

4 Click Back up files.

5 Choose a place to save your back-up. Click Next.

6 Select what to back up. First timers should select everything. Click Next.

7 Choose settings for how often, what day and what time future back-ups should occur.

8 Click Save settings and start backup.

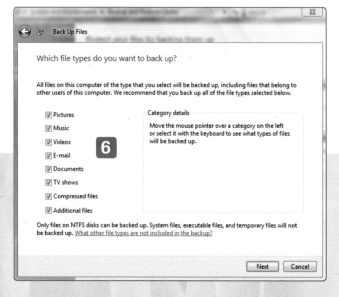

 **HOT TIP:** Since back-ups can be large, consider using a USB drive, external hard drive or DVD. You can also choose a network location.

? DID YOU KNOW?
You can't create a back-up on the hard disk of the laptop that you are backing up.

? DID YOU KNOW?
You may be prompted to insert a blank DVD or insert a USB drive, depending on the choice you made in step 5.

12 Travelling with a laptop

Introduction

The main reason you have a laptop may very well be because it's a mobile device. You may want to take it with you when you travel for work and pleasure. Being mobile brings its own set of problems, though, including getting through airport security, having to leave the laptop in a car or hotel room and dealing with customs, to name just a few. In this chapter you'll learn how to avoid common problems, keep your laptop secure and use your laptop safely.

Back up your laptop before you leave

If your laptop is your only computer, you probably have everything of any importance on it. Some of the data may be precious to you, such as family photos, and some may be sensitive, such as tax information and personal or business documents. When travelling with a laptop, you have to be sure you back up your data carefully.

1 Make a back-up copy of all your important files, including what's on your desktop and in your personal folders.

2 Be sure to back up pictures and videos.

3 Store the back-up on an external drive, which you should leave at home.

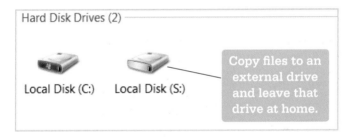

Hard Disk Drives (2)

Local Disk (C:)   Local Disk (S:)

Copy files to an external drive and leave that drive at home.

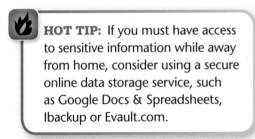

HOT TIP: If you must have access to sensitive information while away from home, consider using a secure online data storage service, such as Google Docs & Spreadsheets, Ibackup or Evault.com.

Clean up your laptop before going on a trip

After the back-up is complete, remove sensitive information from your laptop. This may include but is not limited to tax spreadsheets, confidential company files, confidential personal files, medical information and similar data.

1 Locate a file or folder to delete.

2 Right-click the file.

3 Choose Delete.

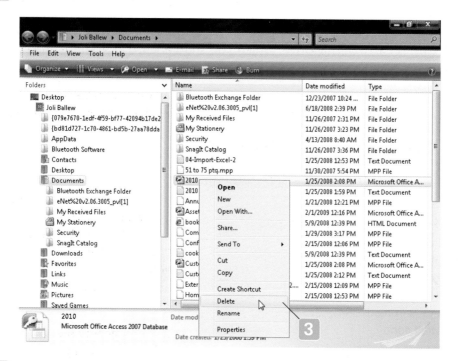

4 Remove, store and leave at home unnecessary external hardware such as webcams, printers, external drives, Ethernet cables and mice.

HOT TIP: When you get back home, you can copy the data from the back-up device to the laptop.

Be sure you need your laptop

Before you travel, you should remove sensitive data off your laptop and onto a USB stick or other back-up device. This way, if your laptop is lost or stolen, whoever ends up with it won't also have access to your sensitive data.

1. Are you staying with relatives?

2. Are you staying in a place with lots of noise? You probably won't get much work done if so.

3. Is your itinerary so filled that you won't have time to use the laptop?

4. If you will have a computer available to you, can you simply take the files you need on a USB stick or CD?

5. Do you need Internet access to work? If so, do you have an Internet service or are there free Internet café's available?

6. Are you going to be too busy camping, swimming, hiking and biking to use your laptop? You can always upload and email the pictures you take once you get home.

7. How far are you going to have to carry your laptop bag?

8. Will you have enough time to get through security with your laptop?

9. Do you have the necessary power adapters if going overseas? If not, can you afford to purchase the required adapters?

 HOT TIP: Sometimes you can use your mobile phone or a small handheld mobile device such as a PDA instead of a laptop.

 HOT TIP: If you're staying with relatives, call ahead to see whether you can use their computer to go online and check email, if that's all you really need to do.

 ALERT: Check to see whether there are any problems taking a laptop through customs in your part of the world. Some require proof of purchase.

Move sensitive data off the laptop

Sometimes you can simply take your data with you on a USB stick, and then access the data from a relative's or business associate's computer. A USB stick is certainly easier to carry than a laptop.

1 Insert the USB stick into one of the laptop's USB ports.

2 Right-click any data you want to move.

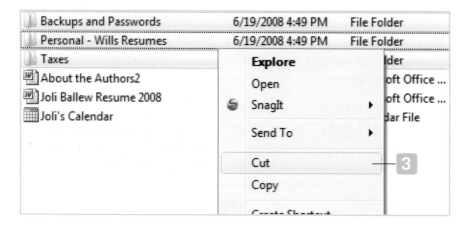

3 Click Cut.

4 Browse to the location to move the file.

5 Right-click and choose Paste.

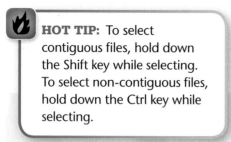

HOT TIP: To select contiguous files, hold down the Shift key while selecting. To select non-contiguous files, hold down the Ctrl key while selecting.

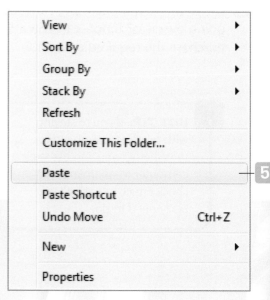

Pack your laptop

If you've decided you need to take your laptop on your trip with you and that you'll have time to use it, you'll want to make sure you pack all of the required accessories, and that you pack correctly.

1 Purchase or borrow a single, heavily padded carrying bag or case that will hold everything you need for your laptop.

2 The bag should have padding, but it should also have compartments to stop the bits of hardware hitting each other.

3 Consider using a backpack on wheels to disguise what you're carrying and discourage theft. It doesn't look like a laptop-carrying case; it looks like a backpack.

4 Make sure you take your power cable, wireless network card, Ethernet cable (in case WiFi is not available) and a USB stick for back-up.

5 Make sure you take power adapters, a plastic bag or something similar to wrap your laptop bag in if you have to walk in the rain with it, and a laptop lock if your laptop offers support for one.

 HOT TIP: Make sure that the bag you choose can also hold any required hardware, such as power cables, an extra battery, an Ethernet cable and a wireless network card.

 HOT TIP: Getting through airport security with a laptop requires you to take it out of the bag, so you'll want to make removing the laptop a quick and easy process.

 HOT TIP: Take an extra battery if you'll be going on long excursions without power.

 HOT TIP: If needed, take a mouse, external keyboard, headset, webcam and surge protector.

Prepare for airline travel

Since 9/11, airports across the globe have tightened security. You have to take off your shoes, belts and jewellery, and place your mobile phone, laptop and other electronic devices in a special bin to be X-rayed. You may also be asked to turn on your laptop to prove it is a working device.

1 Purchase a heavily padded carrying case, preferably with wheels so you can pull it behind you.

2 Pack the case carefully, placing the laptop in a compartment by itself for easy removal.

 HOT TIP: Make sure all your required peripherals will fit in the bag, such as power cables, network cards and Ethernet cables.

3 If you have to work on an aeroplane but can't get access to a power outlet, carry an extra battery on the plane with you.

4 Remove disks from disk drives.

5 If you are unsure what type of power adapter to take, call the airline or the accommodation where you plan to stay.

 HOT TIP: Purchase the proper adapter and pack it before leaving.

6 Call your accommodation in advance to find out how you can connect to the Internet while you're staying there.

7 Call your insurance company and ask whether your laptop will be covered on your trip.

8 Charge your laptop battery completely before leaving for the airport.

9 Avoid having your laptop stolen by monitoring it closely.

10 If possible, keep your laptop at your feet during the flight.

 HOT TIP: You may need to take a phone cord for dial-up, an Ethernet cable for wired connections, or a wireless network card for satellite service.

 DID YOU KNOW? It's safe to put your laptop through an X-ray machine.

Account for time zone differences

Once you've arrived at your destination, left the plane and reached your accommodation, you should change the time and time zone settings on your laptop.

1 Click Start.

2 Click Control Panel.

3 Click Clock, Language and Region.

4 To change the time zone, click Change the time zone.

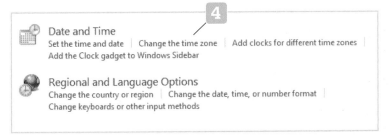

5 Click Change time zone.

6 Select the time zone from the drop-down list.

7 Click OK.

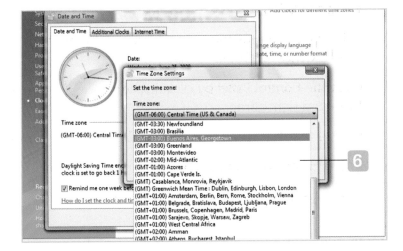

 HOT TIP: With the Date and Time window still open, click Change date and time to change these options.

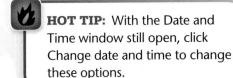 **HOT TIP:** To add clocks, click the Additional Clocks tab.

Change the default language

You can change the country or region so that information you obtain online matches your current location.

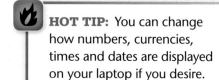
1. Open Control Panel.

2. Click Clock, Language and Region.

3. Click Regional and Language Options.

4. From the Formats tab, click Customize this format if you want to change the number, currency, time or date settings.

5. There are myriad options. Make your changes and click OK.

6. Click the Location tab to select a new location.

7. From the drop-down list, select your present location.

8. Continue configuration as warranted. Click OK when finished.

9. Close the Control Panel by clicking the X in the top right corner.

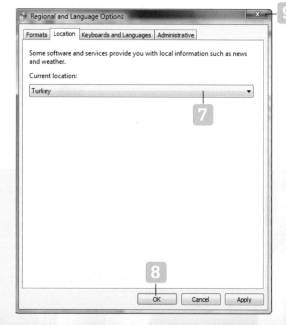

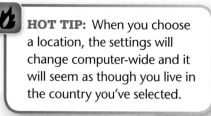

Stay safe online

During your travels you need to take as many precautions as possible when you're online, especially if you're in a public place such as an Internet café. There is no way for you to know whether the connection you have to the Internet is safe or whether others can access your laptop while you're online.

1 When prompted to connect to a public network, make sure you select Public.

2 Make sure your laptop's security applications and software updates are current, including antivirus software, firewall and antispyware.

3 Limit the amount of confidential information you send over the Internet. If possible, do not make credit-card purchases or travel reservations, or input your National Insurance number.

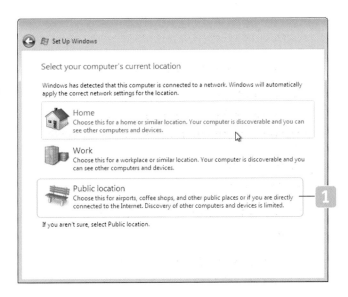

4 Always sign out of any secure website you enter, so that the next person can't use your information to make purchases or withdraw funds.

5 If possible, delete your browsing history. In Internet Explorer 7, you'll find this option under Tools.

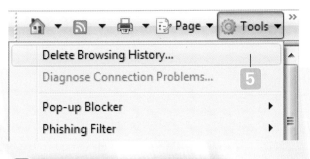

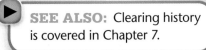

SEE ALSO: Clearing history is covered in Chapter 7.

HOT TIP: Set up a remote webmail account to enable email access from any browser, such as Gmail, Yahoo! Mail or MSN Hotmail. Webmail servers have built-in security that you can benefit from while travelling.

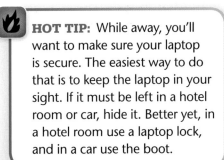

HOT TIP: While away, you'll want to make sure your laptop is secure. The easiest way to do that is to keep the laptop in your sight. If it must be left in a hotel room or car, hide it. Better yet, in a hotel room use a laptop lock, and in a car use the boot.

13 Maintain your laptop

Introduction

There are a few things you have to do to keep your laptop in tip-top shape for the long term. One is to physically clean the laptop, but it's important to note you can't just scrub it down with soap and water. You have to know what to do and how to do it so that you don't harm any of the laptop components. You also need to maintain your laptop by using surge protections and backing up data.

Clean the outside

Your laptop may look just fine, except for a few fingerprints or a couple of sticky spots on the outside of the case. However, the case does need attention every now and again. You'll need to clear the external ports of dust and the keyboard of food particles, and tidy up and remove any other unwanted dirt and grime.

 ALERT: Since it's important to keep these areas dirt-free, you should perform steps to clean these areas two to three times a year, or as needed.

1 Click Start.

2 Click the arrow shown at the bottom of the Start menu.

3 Click Shut Down.

4 Unplug the laptop from the wall outlet.

5 Disconnect all external hardware, including external webcams, flash drives and printers.

6 Use a vacuum cleaner with a small attachment to pull dust from the external ports. If there is an air intake, clean that as well.

7 Use compressed air to blow out remaining dust and dirt.

8 Clean any additional crevices with a dry cotton swab.

9 Clean the plastic outside of the tower with a cotton rag sprayed with a mild non-abrasive cleaner. Do not get any electrical parts or ports wet.

HOT TIP: For tough spots, add a touch of vinegar to a soft, non-abrasive cleaning cloth.

10 Reconnect the peripherals.

Clean the keyboard and monitor

When you clean the inside of a laptop you have to deal with two things: the monitor and the keyboard.

1 Shut down the laptop and unplug it.

2 Use a soft, dry, non-abrasive cloth to clean the monitor.

3 To clean the keyboard, hold the entire laptop upside down with the lid open and shake gently.

4 Turn the laptop right side up, and use a toothpick to loosen any dirt stuck between the keys.

ALERT: When cleaning the laptop screen, make sure you read any instructions that came with your laptop. There may be specific instructions you need to follow when cleaning the screen.

ALERT: Never spray anything directly on to the monitor.

ALERT: Don't use a paper towel to clean the monitor. If possible, purchase an LCD cleaning cloth kit.

 HOT TIP: With help, use compressed air to remove additional dust and grime from the keyboard.

Apply surge protection

Lightning strikes, electrical power surges and power outages can wreak havoc on your laptop's power supply and internal parts. One big lightning strike can destroy a laptop, as can a blast from a personal generator or your city's over-taxed electrical grid. To be safe, when your laptop is plugged in, it should be connected to a surge protector, which often comes in the form of a power strip.

1 Purchase a surge protector. Make sure you do not purchase a simple power strip.

2 Plug in the laptop's electrical cord to the laptop.

 ALERT: Power strips don't offer protection – they only offer additional electrical outlets.

HOT TIP: Also plug in modems, printers and other hardware.

WHAT DOES THIS MEAN?

Surges: Unexpected increases in the voltage of an electrical current. Surges have the potential to damage sensitive electrical equipment. Sags are the equally dangerous opposite of surges – they are a drop in electrical current.

Back up a folder to an external drive

Once you have your data saved in folders, you can copy the folders to an external drive in order to create a back-up. You copy the folder to the external drive in the same way that you'd copy a folder to another area of your hard drive: you open both folders and then drag and drop.

1 Click Start and click Computer.

2 Locate the external drive. Leave this window open.

3 Locate a folder to copy.

> **HOT TIP:** Click Start and click your personal folder (the one with your name on it) to locate a folder to copy.

> **ALERT:** Before you begin, plug in and attach the external drive.

> **HOT TIP:** Small USB flash drives make great back-up devices.

4 Position the windows so you can see them both.

5 Right-click the folder to copy.

6 While holding down the right mouse key, drag the folder to the new location.

7 Drop it there.

8 Choose Copy Here.

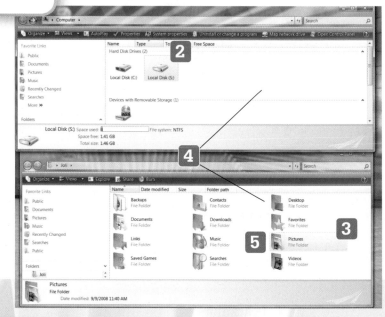

> **ALERT:** Don't choose Move Here. This will move the folder off the laptop and on to the hard drive.

14 Fix problems

Introduction

When problems arise, you will want to resolve them quickly. Vista offers plenty of help. System Restore can fix problems automatically by restoring your laptop to an earlier time. You can use the Network and Sharing Center to help you resolve connectivity problems and use Device Manager to roll back a new driver that doesn't work.

Enable System Restore

System Restore, if enabled, regularly creates and saves restore points that contain information about your laptop that Windows uses to work properly. If your laptop starts acting oddly, you can use System Restore to restore your laptop to a time when the laptop was working properly.

1. Click Start.

2. In the Start Search box, type System Restore.

3. Click System Restore under the Programs results.

4. Click Open System Protection.

5. Verify that the C: drive, or the System drive, is selected. If it is not, select it.

6. Click OK.

7. In the System Restore window, click Cancel.

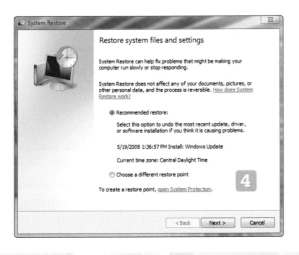

ALERT: System Restore can't be enabled unless the laptop has at least 300 MB of free space on the hard disk, or if the disk is smaller than 1 GB.

? DID YOU KNOW?
You can create a restore point manually by clicking Create.

ALERT: Create a restore point manually any time you think you're about to do something that may cause the laptop harm, such as downloading and installing a third-party application.

WHAT DOES THIS MEAN?

Restore point: A snapshot of the Registry and system state that can be used to make an unstable laptop stable again.

Registry: A part of the operating system that contains information about hardware configuration and settings, user configuration and preferences, software configuration and preferences, and other system-specific information.

Use System Restore

When a problem occurs on your laptop, your first step to resolving the problem is often System Restore. Use System Restore when you download or install software or hardware that causes a problem for the laptop, or any time the laptop seems unstable.

1 Open System Restore.

2 Click Next to accept and apply the recommended restore point.

3 Click Finish.

> **?** DID YOU KNOW?
> System Restore is a system utility. It can't recover a lost personal file, email or picture.

> **!** ALERT: If your laptop has a virus, System Restore probably won't work to resolve the problem, as viruses often attack personal files as well as system files.

> **!** ALERT: If you're running System Restore on a laptop, make sure the laptop is plugged in. System Restore should never be interrupted.

> **?** DID YOU KNOW?
> Because System Restore works only with its own system files, running System Restore will not affect any of your personal data. Your pictures, email, documents, music etc. will not be deleted or changed.

Resolve Internet connectivity problems

When you have a problem connecting to your local network or to the Internet, you can often resolve the problem in the Network and Sharing Center.

1 Open the Network and Sharing Center.

2 Click the red X.

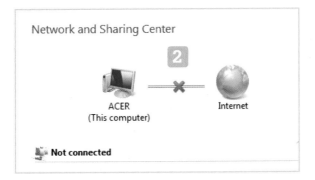

3 Perform the steps in the order they are presented.

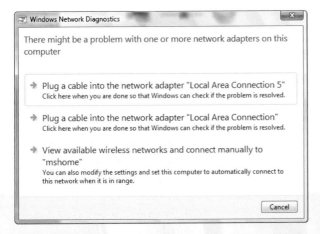

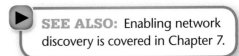
ALERT: Make sure your modem, router, cables and other hardware are properly connected, plugged in and turned on.

SEE ALSO: Enabling network discovery is covered in Chapter 7.

ALERT: You won't see a red X if the network is functioning properly.

ALERT: If prompted to reset your broadband or satellite connection, turn off all hardware, including the laptop, and restart them in the following order: cable/satellite/DSL modem, router, laptops.

DID YOU KNOW?
Almost all of the time, performing the first step will resolve your network problem.

ALERT: When restarting a cable or satellite modem, remove any batteries to completely turn off the modem.

Use Device Driver Rollback

If you download and install a new driver for a piece of hardware and it doesn't work properly, you can use Device Driver Rollback to return to the previously installed driver.

1. Click Start.

2. Right-click Computer.

3. Click Properties.

> **ALERT:** You can only roll back to the previous drive. This means that if you install a driver (D1) and it doesn't work, and then you install another driver (D2) and it doesn't work, using Device Driver Rollback will revert to D1, not the driver before it.

> **SEE ALSO:** Downloading and installing a driver are covered in Chapter 5.

> **ALERT:** The Roll Back driver option will be available only if a new driver has recently been installed.

4. Under Tasks, click Device Manager (not shown).

5. Click the + sign next to the hardware that uses the driver you want to roll back to.

6. Double-click the device name.

7. Click the Driver tab.

8. Click Roll Back driver.

9. Click OK.

> **ALERT:** You may have to restart your laptop.

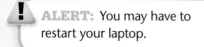

Reconnect loose cables

Many problems occur due to loose or disconnected cables. A mouse can't work unless the mouse or its wireless component is plugged in. A cable modem can't work unless it's connected securely to the laptop and the wall outlet. When troubleshooting, always check your connections.

1 Locate the hardware device that is not working.

2 Follow the cord to verify that it is connected to a power source, if required.

3 Follow any cables from the device to the laptop to verify that it is connected securely.

4 Restart the laptop if the hardware does not begin to work within a few seconds.

! ALERT: If you aren't sure whether a cable is properly inserted, remove it and reinsert it.

? DID YOU KNOW?
Many bits of hardware have multiple connections and connection types. If one type of connection doesn't work, try another, e.g. FireWire instead of USB.

View available hard drive space

Problems can occur when the laptop's hard drive space gets too low. This can become a problem when you use a laptop to record television shows or movies (these require a lot of hard drive space), or if your hard drive is partitioned.

WHAT DOES THIS MEAN?

Partition: Some hard drives are configured to have multiple sections, called partitions. The C: partition may have 20 GB available, while the D: partition may have 60 GB. If you save everything to the C: partition (failing to use the D: partition), it can get full quickly.

---

1 Click Start.

2 Click Computer.

3 In the Computer window, click the C: drive.

4 View the available space.

ALERT: If you find you are low on disk space, you'll have to delete unnecessary files and applications.

ALERT: If the drive is more than 85% full, delete or move some of the data on it, if possible.

HOT TIP: If you see a second drive, as shown here, click it too; you may find you can move data from the C: drive to the second drive to recover much needed space on the C: drive.

Uninstall unwanted programs

If you haven't used an application in more than a year, you probably never will. You can uninstall unwanted programs from Control Panel.

ALERT: Your laptop may have come with programs you don't even know about. Perform the steps listed here to find out.

1 Click Start, and then click Control Panel.

2 In Control Panel, click Uninstall a program.

3 Scroll through the list. Click a program name if you want to uninstall it.

4 Click Uninstall/Change.

5 Follow the prompts to uninstall the program.

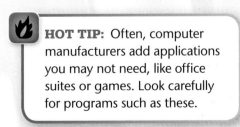

HOT TIP: Often, computer manufacturers add applications you may not need, like office suites or games. Look carefully for programs such as these.

Top 10 Laptop Problems Solved

Problem 1: I can't start my laptop

You need to plug in the laptop and recharge the batteries, locate the power button, insert the battery and view the battery status.

1 If the battery is not connected to the laptop, connect it:

    (a) Carefully turn the laptop upside down and place it on a desk or table.

    (b) Locate the battery bay and open it.

    (c) Unlatch the battery latch.

    (d) Install the battery.

    (e) Lock the battery into place.

    (f) Secure the latch.

    (g) Close the battery bay door.

2 Locate the power cord. It may consist of two pieces that need to be connected.

3 Connect the power cord to the back or side of the laptop, as noted in the documentation. You may see a symbol similar to the one shown here.

4 Plug the power cord into the wall outlet.

5 Open the laptop's lid and press the Power button.

6 Open Mobility Center. (Click Start, and in the Start Search window type Mobility.)

7 Click the arrow to view the three power plans: Balanced, Power saver and High performance. Pick one.

8 View the current status of the battery life.

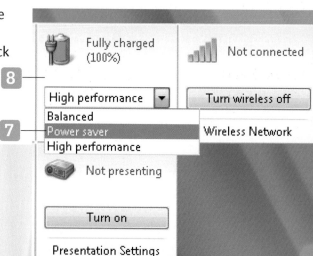

Problem 2: I am at a free wireless hotspot but I don't see any network that I can connect to

You need to enable wireless connectivity or turn on Network discovery.

Open Mobility Center.

Click Turn wireless off to disable WiFi.

Click Turn wireless on to enable it.

Open the Network and Sharing Center.

Under Sharing and Discovery, click the down arrow next to Off by Network discovery. It will become an upwards arrow.

Click Turn on network discovery unless it is already turned on.

Click Apply.

Click the X to close the Network and Sharing Center.

Problem 3: I can't upload photo from my digital camera

You need to install the camera and then connect it and wait for the prompts to uploa the images.

1 Read the directions that come with the camera. If there are specific instructions fo installing the driver, follow them. If not, continue here.

2 Connect the camera to a wall outlet or insert fresh batteries.

3 Connect the camera to the PC using either a USB cable or a FireWire cable.

4 With the camera connected, if nothing happens, turn the camera on.

5 When prompted, choose Import Pictures using Windows.

6 Type a descriptive name for the group of pictures you're importing.

7 Click Import.

Problem 4: I can't connect to the Internet

You can use the troubleshooters in Vista to find out why.

Open the Network and Sharing Center.

To diagnose a non-working Internet connection, click Diagnose and repair.

Click the first solution to resolve the connectivity problem.

Often, the problem is resolved. If it is not, move to the next step and then the next, until it is resolved.

Click the X in the top right corner of the Network and Sharing Center window to close it.

ALERT: If you are connected to the Internet, you will see a green line between your computer and the Internet. If you are not connected, you will see a red X.

Problem 5: I'm getting way too much junk email (spam). What can I do?

Enable the junk email filter in Windows Mail.

1️⃣ Click Tools.

2️⃣ Click Junk E-mail Options.

3️⃣ From the Options tab, make a selection. We suggest starting at Low and moving to High if necessary later.

4️⃣ Click the Phishing tab.

5️⃣ Select Protect my Inbox from messages with potential Phishing links. Additionally, move phishing email to the Junk E-mail folder.

6️⃣ Click OK.

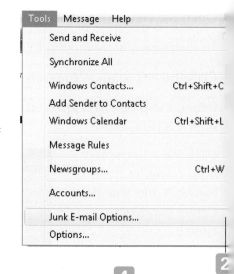

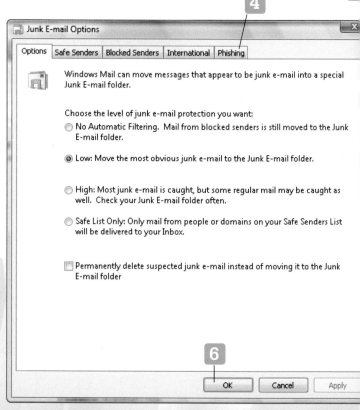

Problem 6: Windows Mail is getting slower and slower. What can I do?

You need to delete unwanted and unnecessary emails from the Sent folder, the Junk E-mail folder and the Deleted Items folder, among others.

Right-click Junk E-mail.

Click Empty 'Junk E-mail' Folder.

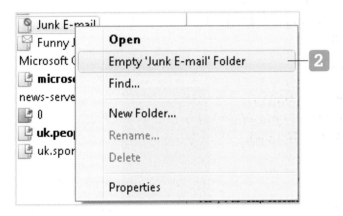

Open the Sent Items folder.

Click Edit and Select All.

Hit the Delete key on the keyboard.

Right-click Deleted Items.

Click Empty 'Deleted Items' Folder.

Problem 7: My computer doesn' do what I want it to do when I insert a blank CD, a DVD movi or a music CD

You can tell Vista what you want it to do when you insert or access media by changin the Autoplay settings.

1 Click Start.

2 Click Default Programs. (It's on the Start menu.)

3 Click Change AutoPlay settings.

4 Use the drop-down lists to select the program to use for the media you want to play.

5 Click Save.

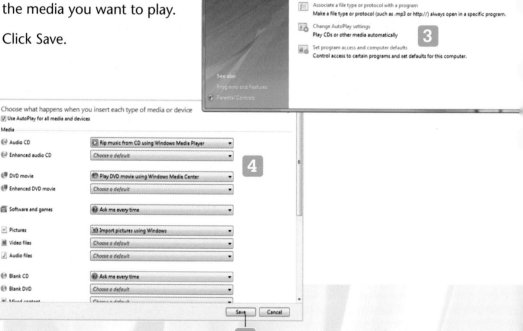

Problem 8: The touchpad on my laptop moves the cursor too fast or too slow. How can I change the speed of the touchpad response time?

You need to make changes to the settings in Control Panel.

Click Start, and in the Start Search window type mouse.

In the results, under Programs click Mouse.

From the Buttons tab, read the options and make the changes as desired.

From the Pointers tab, select a theme if desired.

From the Pointer Options tab, read the options and make the changes as desired.

From the Wheel tab, read the options and make the changes as desired.

Click OK.

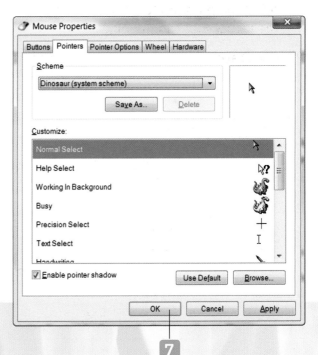

7

HOT TIP: If you're not happy with how fast the pointer moves when you move your mouse, you can change that speed here.

Problem 9: I think I have a virus. How can I find out?

Use Windows Defender to scan your laptop.

1 Click Start.

2 Click Control Panel.

3 Click Security.

4 Click Windows Defender.

Windows Defender
Scan for spyware and other potentially unwanted software

5 Click the arrow next to Scan (not the Scan icon). Click Full Scan if you think the laptop has been infected.

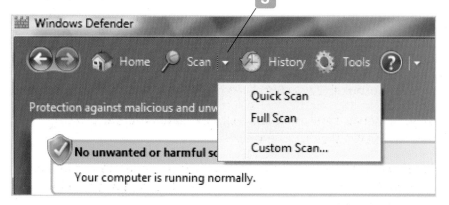

6 Click the X in the top right corner to close the Windows Defender window.

Problem 10: I want to be safe while travelling with my laptop, but I'm not sure what I can do

You need to be aware of certain precautions you can take to protect your laptop, yourself and your data.

- Make a back-up copy of all your important files, including what's on your desktop and in your personal folders.

- Be sure to back up pictures and videos.

- Store the back-up on an external drive, which you leave at home.

- Purchase or borrow a single, heavily padded carrying bag or case that will hold everything you need for your laptop.

- Make sure the bag you choose has padding. It should also have compartments to stop the different bits of hardware from hitting each other.

- Consider using a backpack on wheels to disguise what you're carrying and discourage theft. It doesn't look like a laptop carrying case; it looks like a backpack.

- Make sure you take your power cable, wireless network card, Ethernet cable (in case WiFi is not available) and a USB stick for back-up.

- Make sure you take power adapters, a plastic rubbish bag or something similar to wrap your laptop bag in if you have to walk in the rain with it, and a laptop lock if your laptop offers support for one.